green guide

PARROTS

OF AUSTRALIA

Terence Lindsey
Series Editor: Louise Egerton

First published in 1998 by
New Holland Publishers (Australia) Pty Ltd
Sydney • London • Cape Town

14 Aquatic Drive, Frenchs Forest NSW 2086, Australia
24 Nutford Place, London W1H 6DQ, United Kingdom
80 McKenzie Street, Cape Town 8001, South Africa

Publishing General Manager: Jane Hazell
Publisher: Averill Chase
Project Manager: Fiona Doig
Series Editor: Louise Egerton
Design and Cartography: Mark Seabrook, Laurence Lemmon-Warde
Picture Researcher: Bronwyn Rennex
Reproduction by DNL Resources
Printed and bound in Singapore by Tien Wah Press

National Library of Australia Cataloguing-in-Publication Data
    Lindsey, Terence, 1941–
    Parrots of Australia
    Includes index

    ISBN 1 86436 306 1

    1. Parrots — Australia. 2. Parrots — Australia. I. Title.
    (Series: Green guide.)
    598.710994

Photographic Acknowledgments
Abbreviations: NHIL = New Holland Image Library; NF = Nature Focus; LT = Lochman
Transparencies; TAPA = Terra Australis Photo Agency.
Photograph positions: t = top; b = bottom; c = centre; m = main; i = inset; l = left; r = right.
S**haen Adey/NHIL**: p. 14r, 19b, 60t, 68t, 88b; **Esther Beaton/TAPA**: p. 8–9, 26t; **Carl Bento/NF**:
p. 56b; **Graeme Chapman**: front cover cr, back cover b, p. 5t, 7, 10t, 11b 13m&i, 16, 23t&b, 27t,
28–29, 29i, 31b, 36t, 42t, 51t, 52–53, 74t, 76, 78b, 81t, 84, 94b; **Brian Chudleigh**: p. 68b, 71; **Paul
Daniels/GEO**: front flap, contents, p. 4, 24m, 33, 86; ***compliments of* the Environment
Australia Biodiversity Group**: p. 49b; **CB &DW Frith**: p. 6t, 15t, 17t, 64–65, 67, 87t; **Tom &
Pam Gardner**: p. 18b, 26t, 30t, 48t, 54, 58b, 65i, 66m&i, 69b; **GEO**: p. 39b, 59t, 61t, 67t, 74b;
CA Henley: front cover b, p. 30b, 37b, 38, 75; **Jiri Lochman**: p. 10b, 12, 15b, 17b, 18t, 19t, 20,
21b, 22, 24i, 25m&i, 26b, 40–41, 45i, 53i, 56t, 57t, 60b, 80, 85, 91m; **Geoff Longford/GEO**: p. 6b,
11t, 46; **Peter Marsack/LT**: front cover t, p. 57t, 78t, 79; **Michael Morcombe**: p. 14l, 34, 35, 39t,
43t&b, 44, 47, 59b, 62t&b, 63b, 87b; **National Library of Australia**: p. 27b, 69t, 88t, 93; **Mike
Provic/Wetro Pics**: p. 31t, 70; **Len Robinson**: front cover cl, p. 35, 41i, 45m, 51b, 73i, 77, 81b, 82,
83, 89b, 91i, 92; **Dennis Sarson/LT**: p. 21t; **L&O Schick/NF**: p. 94t; **Raoul Slater/LT**: p. 49t; **Gary
Steer/TAPA**: p. 72–73; **T. Tucker**: back flap; **Dave Watts/Wild Images**: back cover t, p. 9i, 32, 37t,
42b, 48b, 49t, 50, 55, 58t, 61b, 63, 89t, 90.

CONTENTS

An Introduction to Parrots

※

*P*arrots are colourful and conspicuous birds. It is difficult to take a stroll in any city park or drive any of the highways of Australia without encountering at least one species of parrot. This book is an introductory guide to the parrots of Australia. It explains how to identify one from another and presents some of the details of their fascinating lives and curious behaviour.

What is a Parrot?

Parrots belong to a group of birds known as Psittaciformes. They have no close relatives except, distantly, the pigeons and doves. Most parrots are brightly coloured, vegetarian and live in flocks. They mate for life, nest usually in tree holes and most seldom migrate. Most, too, lack the ability to make musical calls; they are nevertheless very vocal, often squawking and twittering as they feed and fly together. Technically two features set them apart from all other birds: one is a short, deep, down-curved bill that looks a bit like that of a bird of prey and the other is the arrangement of their toes, with two pointing forward and the other two pointing backwards. Some other birds have similar feet but it is the combination of these two features that is unique to parrots.

'The Land of Parrots'

Australia has been labelled often as 'the land of parrots' and the continent indeed has more parrot species than almost any comparable region on Earth. Worldwide there are some 332 species, of which about 55 occur in Australia. Many of Australia's parrots are abundant and, because they are easy to see, they make up a conspicuous part of the country's complement of approximately 750 bird species. There are however a few very rare Australian parrots, among them the Orange-bellied and Princess Parrots.

Australia is also the heart of that part of the world where all three major 'clusters' of parrot types – cockatoos, lorikeets and 'typical' parrots – can be found.

A male Australian King-Parrot. Parrots are often brightly coloured and all have deep, curved bills.

4

Many parrots are strongly gregarious, like these Rainbow Lorikeets at a feeding tray.

The Three Lineages

The most sophisticated DNA tests available indicate that cockatoos are markedly different from other parrots. To reflect this they are often placed in a separate family, the Cacatuidae.

The lorikeets are also considered slightly different but somewhat less so; they are generally treated as a subfamily of the main parrot family, Psittacidae.

Among the typical parrots, the grass parrots and the rosellas stand out as especially distinct and, purely for convenience, we have organised these, as well as the the 'offshore' and 'other' parrots, under separate headings: all are members of the typical parrot group.

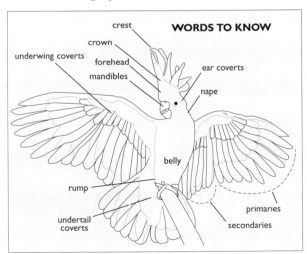

WORDS TO KNOW

crest
crown
underwing coverts
forehead
mandibles
ear coverts
nape
belly
rump
primaries
undertail coverts
secondaries

Where do Parrots Live?

Golden-shouldered Parrots inhabit open tropical woodlands on Cape York Peninsula, wherever there are abundant termite mounds for nesting.

*P*arrots occupy almost all tropical habitats, from lowland rainforests to the harshest of deserts; some inhabit the seashore and a few even occur in high mountains. Most live in trees but there are at least three exceptions: the Ground Parrot and Night Parrot of Australia and the Kakapo of New Zealand; these parrots live only on the ground.

Parrots are almost cosmopolitan although they have a strong bias for the Southern Hemisphere. They range south as far as Tierra del Fuego and north to Afghanistan. Scores of species occupy the lowland tropical rainforests of Brazil and New Guinea but a few reach even the most remote of islands, such as Auckland and Macquarie in the subantarctic and tiny Henderson Island in the central Pacific. In Australia they occur from the Indian Ocean to the eastern seaboard and from Tasmania to the tip of Cape York Peninsula. From tropical mangrove swamps to sandy deserts and from alpine heaths to dense rainforests, there is always at least one species of parrot to be seen.

Why do So Many Parrots form Flocks?

*W*hether foraging is best carried out alone or in the company of others depends very much on the food resource and how it is distributed. Insects, for example, are most efficiently harvested alone but where seeds are abundant they can often be readily gathered in the company of others. Parrots and cockatoos are largely seed-eaters so competition between individuals for food is comparatively low and they can afford to exploit the advantages of flocking behaviour. Large flocks mean many eyes, both to find more food supplies and to keep a sharp lookout for danger. More complex social behaviour is also possible in flocks: Sulphur-crested Cockatoos and several other cockatoos, for example, post sentries in nearby treetops to watch for danger while the rest of the flock forages on the ground.

A Corella guard is posted in a nearby tree while the rest of the flock feeds safely on the ground.

Are Parrots Creatures of Habit?

Parrots are creatures of habit; these Galahs stop off for a drink on their nightly homeward flight.

*A*ustralian parrots are remarkably uniform in their daily routines. At dawn the birds awaken and, especially in desert regions, they fly off to a nearby waterhole to drink. After a spell of drinking and preening, the birds scatter to forage, often commuting several kilometres to their feeding areas.

Many Australian parrots take their food largely from the ground but nectar-feeding lorikeets and eucalypt seed-eating cockatoos scour bushes and trees for food.

There are often two feeding sessions per day. The first of these commonly ends around mid-morning, when the birds retire to the nearest trees to while away the hottest hours of the day high in the shady canopy of leaves. This sort of siesta period is spent loafing, dozing and leisurely preening. In the late afternoon they resume foraging. Then, towards sunset they set out on their homeward flight to their roosts, generally stopping off along the way to have a drink.

BIG AND SMALL
The size range among parrots is enormous. The smallest members, the pygmy-parrots of New Guinea, are much smaller than a sparrow. At the other end of the scale, the Hyacinth Macaw of South America exceeds a metre in total length. In this book we indicate the approximate total length of each species of parrot, measured from the tip of the beak to the tip of the tail, next to the heading on the entry for that species.

THE COCKATOOS

Who are the Cockatoos?

Cockatoos are the only members of the parrot group with movable crests. They are large, noisy and gregarious birds, not as brightly coloured as most other parrots.

The cockatoos are best represented in Australia but there are a few species in New Guinea and a few others extend to Indonesia and the Philippines. The largest is the spectacular Palm Cockatoo and the smallest species is the Cockatiel. These two species aside, cockatoos tend to fall into two groups, which might be labelled 'white' and 'black' cockatoos. The 'white' cockatoos are white or nearly so; they are moderately big and feed mainly on the ground in open country. The 'black' cockatoos have mostly black plumage. They are very large, have long tails and are more closely associated with forests and woodlands.

The cockatoos are distinguished from other parrots mainly by their generally larger size, muted colours and conspicuous crests.

What Use is a Dead Tree?

Some of the cockatoos have profited from human change to the environment and have become more common or widespread in the past century or two but most of the parrots, and especially the cockatoos, need deep, roomy cavities in trees in which to nest. It takes a large cavity to satisfy the requirements of a bird as big as, say, a Yellow-tailed Black-Cockatoo. Large cavities usually form only in very big trees. These days, few trees are allowed to reach such a stage. If they grow in forests, they are harvested; if they grow in the suburbs, they are removed for reasons of safety. From a cockatoo's perspective, it comes to the same thing: the cavity disappears along with the tree, which confronts it with a severe housing shortage.

Once established, a pair of Galahs will often use the same tree cavity for nesting all their lives.

How do Cockatoos Breed?

Cockatoos, like most parrots, mate for life and breed in spring. They lay one to six eggs, depending on the species. These the female deposits on a carpet of small wooden fragments in the cavity of a tree. The cavity is usually in a large eucalypt near water, often high and inaccessible. During the nesting period the male feeds his mate and later he helps rear the chicks. Among the black-cockatoos, males usually leave incubation to the female but among white cockatoos this duty is generally shared by both parents. The incubation period is about 24 days and chicks fledge after 56–90 days, large species usually taking longer than smaller ones. Several of the large black-cockatoo species normally rear only one youngster, even when two eggs are laid and hatched.

A black-cockatoo chick takes about 90 days to grow its full complement of feathers.

Where do Flocks of Cockatoos Go?

All of the cockatoos roost communally in trees, drink at dawn, then scatter to forage in small flocks or family parties. They are strong fliers and often commute 20–30 km or more between their roosts and feeding areas. They follow the conventional parrot routine of morning feeding, followed by a siesta in the tree canopy and a couple more hours feeding before returning in flocks to their roost, usually stopping off for a drink on their way home.

A common feature of the cockatoo lifestyle is the nightly congregation in a suitably large tree.

CARELESS COLLECTORS
The housing shortage has been rendered particularly acute because of the cockatoo's popularity as a pet, especially overseas. Chicks in the nest are the most desirable and unscrupulous collectors will often cut trees down as the simplest way of reaching the cavities. This careless action not only results in the loss of a year's brood; it also removes the possibility of many other broods in years to come.

Cockatiel

32 cm

The high pointed crest and bold white wing patches are identifying features of the Cockatiel.

Cockatiels are easy to identify by shape alone, even in silhouette: the combination of slim build, high pointed crest and long, tapering tail is distinctive. Male Cockatiels are mainly very dark grey with yellow faces and an orange patch behind the eye, while females and young birds are generally duller with barred tails and greyish faces. Because these parrots feed mainly on the ground and their grey plumage tends to blend in with the background, foraging flocks of cockatiels are quite easily overlooked. As soon as they take flight, however, large white patches in their wings stand out boldly.

RARE SIGHTINGS

To see a Cockatiel south of about 30°S in winter is rare. The species has been recorded in Tasmania but these are almost certainly escaped cage birds.

Habits, Habitat and Distribution

Occasionally encountered alone or in pairs, especially when breeding, Cockatiels occur more often in large flocks. Their most frequent call is a distinctive, querulous 'queel, queel', delivered with an upward inflection as they fly. When resting, they perch along telephone wires or in large dead trees. The Cockatiel is common and widespread across the interior of Australia but avoids forests and woodlands. Always on the move, its migrations are more or less random but there is a distinct seasonal trend towards the north in winter and towards the south in summer.

Gang-gang Cockatoo

35 cm

The Gang-gang is easily identi-fied by its unique 'feather-duster' crest. In adult males it is red, in females and youngsters it is grey but in both cases the shape is distinctive. Although widespread in forests and woodlands throughout south-eastern Australia, Gang-gangs are most strongly associated with the highland eucalypt forests of the Australian Alps, the Snowy Mountains and the Blue Mountains.

Suburban Cockies

Gang-gangs breed in dense forests but descend to lower altitudes and more open environments in winter in search of food. One of the most conspicuous birds in Canberra's parks and wooded gardens during winter, for example, is the Gang-gang. It is drawn to such suburban areas by its fondness for the fruits and berries of various ornamental shrubs, especially hawthorn.

Behaviour

Like other cockatoos, Gang-gangs usually occur in pairs or family parties but larger flocks often form in winter. Most of their food is taken in trees but they occasionally forage on the ground. They spend much of their day feeding quietly and methodi-cally. Often extraordinarily tame, it

Male and female Gang-gang Cockatoos are very similar except that the male (above) has a red head, while that of the female (left) is grey.

is sometimes possible to approach almost within touching distance. Gang-gangs often utter a distinctive conversational note while feeding: a sort of quiet, gruff, grating screech rather like a rusty hinge on an iron gate.

Do Parrots Make Good Pets?

The Budgerigar ranks as by far the world's most popular avian pet.

Wild parrots are sometimes quite tame; this Crimson Rosella alights on a bemused tourist.

*M*any parrot species are hardy and adaptable, and do well in captivity. Many, too, thrive on a simple diet of seeds, fruit and greens. They make affectionate, intelligent, lively pets and some are very easy to care for. The Budgerigar, for example, was first taken to Europe by John Gould in 1840 and quickly established itself as a firm favourite. It has since become the most widespread of pets, valued virtually throughout the western world for its friendly personality, bright colours and hardiness.

Among the cockatoos, the Cockatiel is nearly as popular as the Budgerigar, and it has also been bred in a wide range of colour mutations including white, pied and pearl. Larger species, such as the Sulphur-crested Cockatoos, can also become very tame and affectionate if reared properly but they are not generally recommended as pets because they are noisy and destructive. All the large cockatoos are much happier when accommodated in a roomy aviary.

A RIPE OLD AGE

Parrots and their kind — especially cockatoos — are exceptionally long-lived birds. Pampered pets sometimes live for 50 years or more and there are several reports of individuals passing the century mark. The oldest wild parrot ever recorded seems to be a Little Corella tagged as an adult in South Australia in 1901 and killed by a car in 1972.

Can Birds Use Tools?

The Palm Cockatoo uses sticks in its courtship display.

*O*nce humans were regarded as the only tool-using animal. Only in the twentieth century has it been discovered that other animals also use tools. Probably the first bird that was known to do so was the Woodpecker Finch of the Galapagos Islands, which in 1901 was found to be using a cactus spine to winkle insects from bark crevices.

The list of birds that use tools is now quite long. In North America, for example, small birds called nuthatches often carry bark pieces from tree to tree. These they use as 'crowbars' to lever bark from tree-trunks in order to reach insects underneath. In Africa, Egyptian Vultures throw stones at Ostrich eggs in order to break them open.

Many captive parrots use tools of various kinds but the Palm Cockatoo's dexterity in its tool use to enhance its courtship displays is particularly remarkable. Males use a chunk of dead wood, a short stick, a large seed or some similar item to batter against their perches while pirouetting and cavorting about on branches. This resonant drumming carries a considerable distance through the forest. Such performances are often given in concert with up to seven birds, especially in the early morning before they scatter to forage.

Why Can Some Parrots Talk ?

*W*hy parrots can mimic the sound of the human voice so successfully is something of a mystery. The talent is all the more remarkable because wild parrots never use it; it manifests itself only in pet birds. Mimicry of natural sounds is not rare among birds but only starlings and their close relatives, the mynas, rival parrots in their ability to imitate human speech. According to laboratory testing, both parrots and starlings rank very high among birds in intelligence. Also both parrots and starlings are strongly sociable in the wild and have the unusual trait among birds of readily forming close and affectionate bonds with humans. It is unlikely that these shared characteristics are a coincidence but what the connection might be remains elusive.

Although noted for their manual dexterity, cockatoos also have a less obvious ability: a remarkable flair for mimicry.

Glossy Black-Cockatoo 48 cm

The Glossy Black-Cockatoo feeds almost exclusively on the seeds of she-oaks.

The Glossy Black-Cockatoo is notable for its extraordinarily rigid diet: it eats almost exclusively the seeds of she-oaks or casuarinas. Plucking one cone at a time from a branch with its bill, the cockatoo holds it in one foot and methodically rotates it, nibbling the seeds as it goes. Only occasionally does it take the seeds of other plants, such as eucalypts, angophoras or wattles, or rip away bark from a trunk to reach insect larvae beneath.

To differentiate Glossy Black-Cockatoos from other black cockatoos, look for the large, irregular patches of yellow on the head of the female. Males are easily confused with the Red-tailed Black Cockatoos since both have panels of bright red in their tails.

Glossy Black-Cockatoos are often extraordinarily tame, allowing an observer to approach within a few metres. Usually small parties feed quietly and methodically in the same casuarina grove all day. Often the only sign of their presence is a soft pattering – almost like raindrops – as discarded seed husks fall from their feet to the ground below. Occasionally one will utter a soft note, midway between a squeal and a grating sound.

Distribution

The Glossy Black-Cockatoo is widespread in southeastern Australia but its dependence on casuarinas means that only certain kinds of forest and woodland suit its needs. It is generally more widespread in coastal areas but it is also common in several of the interior mountain ranges of New South Wales, such as the Cocoparras and the Wedin Range. The population on Kangaroo Island is isolated and the bird is extinct in mainland South Australia.

The Palm Cockatoo is unmistakable.

Palm Cockatoo 56 cm

Largest and most impressive of all the cockatoos are the Palm Cockatoos. They fly in loud, squealing groups over the forest canopy and are fond of perching high in conspicuous trees. Their spectacular shaggy crests and huge bills are distinctive but they are also the only cockatoos with naked, bright red faces. Males and females differ little in appearance.

Palm Cockatoos are widespread in New Guinea and the Aru Islands but in Australia they are confined to the rainforests towards the tip of Cape York Peninsula: here they are common. Although rainforest is their main habitat, they forage over a wide area, often visiting nearby areas of open woodland to feed on seeds and fruits. Like most cockatoos, they gather at night to roost in large trees.

A Red-tailed Black-Cockatoo.

Red-tailed Black-Cockatoo 55–66 cm

The Red-tailed Black-Cockatoo is perhaps even more spectacular than the Palm Cockatoo because it sometimes congregates in flocks of several hundreds of birds. Over much of tropical inland Australia it is the only large black-cockatoo. Though widespread, its distribution tends to follow major river systems, where there are trees suitable for nesting. Its numbers in the south have been drastically reduced since European settlement but it remains common in the north.

The male's plumage is almost entirely black except for panels of bright red in the tail. Females are similar but dusky brown and their panels are mainly yellow. It would be very easy to confuse the male Red-tailed Black-Cockatoo with the male Glossy Black-Cockatoo, except that the two species occupy very different habitats and seldom occur together in the same region.

> **PORTRAIT OF A PARROT**
> The Red-tailed Black-Cockatoo is the subject of the earliest known illustration of an Australian parrot. It is a pencil sketch made by the naturalist Sydney Parkinson who sailed on board Captain James Cook's vessel *The Endeavour* in 1770.

A Tale of Two Cockies

*T*he situation of the two black-cockatoo species in far southwestern Australia is among the most remarkable examples of multiple speciation to be found in birds anywhere in the world. The usual way in which species evolve is by being isolated for a very long time. The isolation might be caused by anything that forms a barrier; it may be a rise in sea level, an up-thrust mountain range or a regional climate change that forms a desert.

The Yellow-tailed Black-Cockatoo once occurred all across southern Australia.

Shrinking Woodland

Once, many thousands of years ago, woodland stretched right across what is now the arid expanse of the Nullarbor Plain and the species we know today as the Yellow-tailed Black-Cockatoo also extended right across southern Australia. However, much later, the climate changed and the average annual rainfall declined. The woodlands retreated accordingly and the cockatoos in the southwest became isolated from those in the southeast as trees disappeared on the intervening Nullarbor Plain. The southwestern birds gradually lost the yellow pigment in their tails and evolved a range of other subtle distinctions, ultimately becoming a distinct species.

A Second Wave

To fully appreciate the black-cockatoo situation in southwestern Australia, you need to exert your imagination a little further and suppose what might the result be if all this happened not once, but on two occasions, a long, long time apart. Astonishingly, the far-fetched answer seems in fact to be this: Eastern Yellow-tailed Black-cockatoos somehow crossed the Nullarbor not once but twice, each time retreating and leaving behind a 'daughter' population that ultimately became a distinct species. And each of the two 'daughter' populations are distinct, not only from their 'parent' population in the east, but also from each other.

Short-billed Black-Cockatoos: one of the two southwestern representatives of the eastern Yellow-tailed Black-Cockatoo.

A Dab Hand at Feeding Etiquette

*T*he Long-billed Black-Cockatoo puts its rather long bill to a very particular and methodical use when dealing with its chief food, the seed-capsules or 'nuts' of karri and marri trees. A feeding bird clutches its perch with one foot while clasping the capsule in the other. With the long pointed tip of its bill it pierces the lid and deftly extracts the seeds one at a time. When the capsule is empty the cockatoo simply discards it by letting it fall and then reaches for another.

ODD MANNERISMS

Oddly, most cockies appear to be left-handed – that is one will usually clutch whatever it is eating in its left foot. Black-cockatoos also have another intriguing and unusual mannerism – they almost invariably back into their nesting cavities tail-first.

A Red-tailed Black-Cockatoo demonstrates its table skills.

Has Farming Affected Parrot Populations?

*F*arming has certainly had a major impact on parrot populations – mainly owing to changes in three resources. At the time of first settlement both the Galah and the Little Corella, for example, were much more restricted in range and vastly less numerous than they are today. Now there are dams or bores for livestock – at which birds can drink, too – every few kilometres across vast areas of Australia's outback. Cereal crops mean large quantities of spilled grain along the roads and railway lines used to transport them: a food bonanza for parrots. Holes for nesting, however, have inexorably declined (see p. 37). Most ground-feeding parrots and cockatoos have been influenced by these factors, although not all to the same degree. One graphic example is the case of the Regent Parrot which, thanks to water and spilled grain, experienced a dramatic population boom with the establishment of the Western Australian wheatbelt but which has since been steadily declining again for years, apparently largely due to a lack of nesting sites.

Farm crops like sunflowers attract parrots and have boosted the populations of some species.

Yellow-tailed Black-Cockatoo

60–70 cm

Large yellow panels in its tail render the Yellow-tailed Black-Cockatoo unmistakable.

The sight of a party of Yellow-tailed Black-Cockatoos flying majestically through the air high above some heavily timbered valley is one of the most impressive that Australia's southern woodlands have to offer. These birds are easily identified by their great size and long tails with large yellow panels. They are widespread and fairly common in the coastal and highland forests of the southeast, roughly from Adelaide to Rockhampton and also Tasmania. Although particularly partial to tall-timbered areas, they often forage on coastal heaths and even in the shrubbery along the median strips of freeways. They spend most of their time in trees, using their massive bills to extract seeds from nuts, fruits and cones, and also to tear bark away from trunks and branches to reach woodboring insect larvae. Strongly arboreal, only seldom do they descend to forage on the ground.

A TASTE FOR THE EXOTIC
The Yellow-tailed Black-Cockatoo is one of the few Australian birds that commonly visits plantations of introduced radiata pine trees to extract the seeds from their cones.

Breeding

Most breeding occurs in spring in the southeast but further north Yellow-tailed Black-Cockatoos breed during winter. After leaving the nest, juvenile birds remain with their parents almost indefinitely and for much of the year the family party is the basic social unit. In the winter however families may congregate together forming large flocks that can involve scores or even hundreds of birds.

A pair of Short-billed Black-Cockatoos.

Short-billed Black-Cockatoo   65 cm

Confined to the far southwest of Australia, the Short-billed Black-Cockatoo very much resembles the Yellow-tailed Black-Cockatoo of the eastern States except in being a little smaller and in having white patches instead of yellow. It feeds either on the ground or in trees and its favourite foods include the seeds of hakeas, banksias and similar plants.

The Short-billed Black-Cockatoo nests mainly in wandoo forests in spring and summer but in winter it roams widely and visits other kinds of woodland as well as coastal heaths. It is common, for example, in Perth and frequently visits suburban gardens to feed. In summer it occurs mainly in pairs or family parties but it often forms large flocks in winter. As in other black-cockatoos, the chief call in flight is high and drawn out, sounding like 'wheee-la', midway between a screech and a whistle.

A Long-billed Black-Cockatoo.

Long-billed Black-Cockatoo   65 cm

Like the Short-billed Black-Cockatoo, the Long-billed Black-Cockatoo is confined to the far southwest of Australia. In winter the two species sometimes occur in the same woodlands and they are virtually impossible to distinguish on appearance. In summer, however, Long-billed Black-Cockatoos mostly confine themselves to karri forests, where they nest.

Although it and the Short-billed Black-Cockatoo are distinct species, the only external difference is its longer and more pointed bill, which it uses to open karri seed capsules, its favourite food. It also sometimes feeds on hakea and banksia seeds and is fond of ripping timber apart to get at large wood-boring grubs. Like its close relative, the Long-billed Black-Cockatoo generally occurs in pairs or parties in summer but sometimes forms large flocks in winter. Both species prefer the highest nest cavities they can find, lay clutches of two eggs and incubate them for about four weeks. Chicks leave the nest in about 90 days.

Which is the Best-known Cockie?

The Sulphur-crested Cockatoo's long, mobile, sulphur-yellow crest is unique among Australian cockatoos.

*T*he Sulphur-crested Cockatoo is probably the most widely known of all cockatoos because it is very common in Australia's heavily populated southeast and around the world it is popular as an affectionate and intelligent, although noisy and destructive, pet. Sulphur-crested Cockatoos have bright, sulphur-yellow crests; their otherwise pure white plumage is suffused with pale yellow on the underwings. Their long, upcurved crest is normally carried sleeked back but it is often raised in interest, alarm or excitement.

The Sulphur-crested Cockatoo is common in forested parts of northern and eastern Australia and it also occurs in New Guinea and parts of Indonesia. It is mainly sedentary, strongly gregarious and eats a wide range of seeds, nuts and fruit. It has a broad vocabulary but its most arresting call is an astonishingly loud, harsh, discordant shriek.

Do Cockatoos Play?

*I*t is difficult to know what else to call a great deal of a cockatoo's normal daily activity. The droll antics of a pair of Galahs on a telephone line, for example, are a common sight along almost any country road. They hang from the wire supported only by their bills, or dangle by one outstretched claw with their wings flapping, or indulge in similar acrobatics that to a human observer look very much like just plain 'foolin' about'. Massed flocks wheel and weave and wend through the trees apparently for the sheer fun of it. And a bored cockie will methodically strip every leaf from a branch held in one foot, seemingly just for something to do. Cockatoos are intelligent, sociable and have a great deal of 'free' time; such activities seem in every way indistinguishable from what we do when we play sport.

Why do Cockatoos Roost Together?

Most cockatoos – in fact most Australian parrots and lorikeets as well – come together in large flocks to spend the night at communal roosts. Sulphur-crested Cockatoos are especially attached to their roosts and seldom abandon them unless forced to move by lack of food, even if the birds must travel tens of kilometres to their feeding grounds.

When these Little Corellas gather in large, chattering flocks in the evenings it is possible that they may be sharing information.

It has often been suggested that one of the functions of such roosts is the opportunity it gives its members to share information about the abundance and location of food supplies. It seems a plausible notion; after all if honeybees can impart such information to their fellows at the hive, a fact long known to beekeepers, surely an intelligent and sociable bird like a cockatoo can manage the same feat. The difficulty is that absolutely nothing is known about how such a means of communication might work.

WINGED VANDALS

Sulphur-crested Cockatoos often come to gardens to be fed but they can cause a great deal of damage to wooden railings, verandas, lead flashing and insulation around wiring with their extraordinarily powerful bills. Home-owners with Sulphur-crested Cockatoos for neighbours are advised not to encourage them to visit by leaving out food.

Galahs are active and playful, and they often practice their acrobatic skills on telephone wires.

Galah

35 cm

Large flocks of Galahs are a common sight in the outback. They usually come to water to drink twice a day.

One of Australia's most abundant birds, the Galah is instantly identifiable by its dove grey back and rosy pink underparts. It has clearly benefited from environmental changes brought about by European settlement. It remains common, or even abundant, over its former range across the interior of the continent, but it has also expanded its range. For example, it is now a common bird in Sydney and several other coastal cities, whereas 20 years ago it did not occur in these places at all. Unusually flexible in its habitat requirements, it is found wherever there is open ground for foraging, tall trees for roosting and suitable tree hollows for nesting.

GENDER DIFFERENCES

In many bird species, males and females differ strikingly in appearance but in others they are hard to tell apart. In fact, the sexes are seldom absolutely identical. Galahs, for instance, differ in eye colour: males have dark brown eyes, while those of females are pinkish red.

Roosting and Feeding

Galahs roost communally but come the morning light they normally drink at the nearest source of water before scattering into smaller groups to feed throughout the day. They may commute as much as 15 kilometres to find suitable food. Their diet is varied but they rely most heavily on the seeds of grasses and similar plants gathered on the ground. In wheat-growing districts, they frequently feed along roadsides, gathering grain spilled from trucks.

Major Mitchell's Cockatoo

32–36 cm

Often known as the Pink Cockatoo, this striking bird with a crest
featuring a unique yellow and
deep salmon pink stripe is a sort
of arid-zone version of the Sulphur-crested Cockatoo. Although
considerably smaller, the two
species are not only similar in
outline but they bear many
resemblances in their behav-
ioural traits. However, where the
Sulphur-crested Cockatoo seems
to have gained ground since
European influence on the land,
Major Mitchell's Cockatoo has
lost it for reasons that are still
not entirely clear. One significant
factor is the inexorable loss of
large old trees for nesting but it
seems likely there are others.

Diet, Distribution and Lifestyle

Major Mitchell's Cockatoos
feed on a diet of seeds, grains,
tubers and similar fare gathered largely on the ground.
They are widespread across
the southern interior of
Australia but patchily distributed. They occur most commonly in mallee, mulga and open
eucalypt or native pine wood-

Australia's loveliest but rarest cockatoo, Major Mitchell's is largely pastel pink, even in very young chicks (inset).

lands and they are usually encountered in small parties,
seldom in large flocks. Like Galahs, young Major Mitchell's Cockatoos spend
several years wandering in a flock before they establish a bond with a mate.

Nesting and Young

Three eggs make up the usual clutch. Like other cockatoos, baby Major
Mitchell's Cockatoos hatch blind and nearly naked and need almost constant
brooding by their parents at first. By about the end of their second week their
eyes are fully open; by the end of their fourth week their feathers have erupted
– although still in their spiky sheaths – and at six weeks they can fly and are
ready to leave the nest.

Who are the Corellas?

*C*orellas are cockatoos with white plumage suffused with pale yellow. They have short crests, pale bills, traces of dull red around the head and neck, and a patch of bare bluish skin around each eye. Noisy and intensely gregarious, they are abundant across much of the arid interior. A large flock of corellas may perch in a dead tree so densely that it looks garlanded in snow: such a sight is one of the most evocative of Australian outback images.

There are, in fact, several different kinds of corellas. As corellas they are easy to identify but sorting out just which one is which can be tricky.

Corellas resemble Sulphur-crested Cockatoos but differ most obviously in their crests. They are also smaller.

How Many Corellas are There?

*T*here are three clusters of populations but whether these are three distinct species remains an open question. Corellas in the north, known as Little Corellas, have rather short, blunt bills; those in the southeast, the Long-billed Corellas, have comparatively long, pointed bills, and so do those in the far southwest, the Western Corellas. In other words, corellas come in three basic types: 'northern short-billed', 'southeastern long-billed' and 'south-western long-billed'. The two southern corella types are probably the descendants of 'marooned' populations that evolved a distinctness as a result of being isolated by deserts that were more extensive than they are now.

The Little Corella is widespread in the interior of Australia but it is far more common in the north than in the south, and two southern populations of its 'long-billed' close relatives are

Confined to parts of the Riverina and western Victoria, the Long-billed Corella is the southeastern representative of the corella clan.

very nearly isolated. The distribution of the south-eastern Long-billed Corellas extends approximately from the Riverina district of New South Wales to the Coorong of South Australia. Its population was severely reduced last century but in recent decades it has shown some signs of recovery and it is now very common in some areas. The Western Corellas are confined to Australia's far southwestern corner.

Western Corellas are confined to far southwestern Australia. Like all corellas, they feed mostly on the ground.

How do Corellas find Water ?

*L*ike cockatoos and other parrots, corellas must drink at least daily and they cannot survive in a desert where there is no water within an hour or two's flying time. Several of Australia's earliest explorers, such as Ludwig Leichhardt,

Ludwig Leichhardt was led to water by corellas.

recorded in their diaries how they were led to life-saving water in the desert by following flocks of corellas and other parrots as they flew to drink. Corellas exploit the advantages of a long life and a strong social tradition in knowing the available sources of water in their environment. Young corellas are led to water by their parents and they learn from others in their years of wandering before they settle down with a mate. In turn they pass on the information to their offspring.

TAKING TO THE COAST
Corellas are mainly birds of the arid interior but since the mid-1960s escaped cage-birds have formed growing populations in several east coastal areas, most notably in Sydney where in some suburbs flocks of several hundreds are now common.

THE LORIKEETS

Who are the Lorikeets?

*T*here are about 55 species of parrots in the group known as the lorikeets or lories. Most are found in New Guinea but there are seven Australian species. These brightly coloured parrots have glossy, compact plumage and brush-tipped tongues. They feed almost exclusively on nectar, occasionally supplemented by pollen, fruit, seeds and insects, and almost never come to the ground. They are intensely gregarious and vocal, keeping in touch with one another by means of a constant chattering and squeaking.

Male and female lorikeets look nearly identical in

Among the more obvious distinctions that set the lorikeets apart are their relatively slender, long, pointed bills.

plumage and young birds differ little from adults. The Varied Lorikeet and the Red-collared Lorikeet are confined to the Top End and the Rainbow Lorikeet and Scaly-breasted Lorikeet are common on the east coast. Three much smaller species, the Musk, Little and Purple-crowned Lorikeets, differ in being most common in the far south – they might be thought of as the 'southern' lorikeets, although there is some overlap.

Lorikeets usually breed in spring and nest in hollows in trees, usually as high as they can find a suitable cavity. The smaller species lay 4–5 plain white eggs, the larger species usually only two. Incubation takes about 21–26 days and the chicks fledge after about 40–55 days. Although the female alone incubates the eggs, both parents feed the chicks and her mate often roosts in the nest with her at night.

The Musk Lorikeet has a moderately long, pointed tail and is largely green, enlivened with patches of red. Like all lorikeets, this species has a relatively slender build.

BRUSH-TIPPED TONGUE

Lorikeets have rather long, fleshy tongues like other parrots but they differ in that the tip of the tongue carries numerous minute, densely-packed, fleshy projections called papillae. These papillae function together rather like a paint-brush, soaking up the nectar from flowers by capillary action. They are also effective in rapidly blotting up pollen.

Why are Nectar-feeders Nomads?

*F*lowering trees represent a food source with three crucial characteristics: they deliver nectar in abundance, but only for a limited time, and at localities widely scattered in space. Animals that exploit such a food source must be prepared to travel long distances in search of it. Lorikeets accordingly are strongly nomadic in habit and they have relatively long, narrow wings well suited to lengthy flights. The birds rocket through the treetops, flying high and fast in small flocks, screeching in their haste.

Like all lorikeets, the Rainbow Lorikeet feeds mainly on nectar.

Is it a Good Idea to Feed Lorikeets?

*M*any urban dwellers in high-rise apartments yield to the temptation of attracting Rainbow Lorikeets to their balcony with food. You might think that a few scraps of sugar-soaked bread on a plain wooden tray strapped to the balcony rail is harmless enough and certainly it will draw a daily congregation of squawking parrots to your home. Unfortunately such handouts are junk food. Although they will happily gorge themselves, this diet is unhealthy for parrots and the more they eat of it, the less inclined they are to search for natural food. The birds also suffer if you go away for a few weeks and their free lunch disappears. By far the best way of attracting birds is to plant native flowering shrubs wherever you can and to provide a shallow tray of clean water somewhere away from the reach of cats.

Rainbow Lorikeets can be attracted to garden bird-feeders easily, but care is needed to ensure a proper diet.

BATHING IN THE TREETOPS

Like other birds, lorikeets need to regularly preen and bathe to keep their plumage in good order. They seldom come to the ground so they do not normally use standing water for bathing. Instead they bathe by vigorously fluttering their wings in dense sprays of foliage soaked by dew or a shower of rain.

Rainbow Lorikeet

30 cm

Striking blue, orange and green plumage makes the Rainbow Lorikeet difficult to mistake for another parrot.

Unmistakable in its vivid finery of deep blue, green, scarlet and yellow, the Rainbow Lorikeet is widespread almost everywhere in eastern Australia from the tip of Cape York Peninsula south to Melbourne and west to Adelaide; occasionally strays find their way to Tasmania. Overseas it also inhabits New Caledonia, Vanuatu, New Guinea and parts of Indonesia. A population in Perth seems to have originated from escaped cage-birds sometime during the late 1960s. Since European settlement populations seem to have declined markedly in the south, remaining truly abundant only from around Sydney northward. Indeed in Sydney and Brisbane it is a most ubiquitous suburban bird and in the tropics it is even more abundant.

Habitat and Habits

Rainbow Lorikeets inhabit most kinds of wooded country, including mangroves, paperbark swamps, rainforests and eucalypt woodlands. They visit a range of flowering trees, both native and introduced, and are especially attracted to flowering coral trees. Gregarious, active and noisy, they can be extremely confident, readily coming to garden feeders in many coastal cities and being quite capable of facing down the much larger Sulphur-crested Cockatoo. At night they roost in large flocks in trees.

Red-collared Lorikeet
30 cm

The Red-collared Lorikeet of the Top End resembles the Rainbow Lorikeet except for its orange nape.

The Red-collared Lorikeet is a close relative of the Rainbow Lorikeet and replaces the latter in the tropics of the Top End and the Kimberley. Related they surely are but just how close that relationship is has been a matter of debate for decades. Some researchers regard them as two distinct species whereas others treat them as merely subspecies, or local populations, of the same species. The most recent studies tend to favour the former view over the latter but the point is far from decided.

Distribution and Making the Distinction

Whether viewed as species or subspecies, the two populations approach each other closely at the head of the Gulf of Carpentaria but they are not known either to overlap or hybridise in the wild. They interbreed readily in captivity but this proves little because very many of Australia's parrot species can be induced to interbreed by skilful manipulation of their captive conditions.

The Red-collared Lorikeet differs most distinctly from the Rainbow Lorikeet in having a conspicuous band of orange-scarlet, broadest at the nape, that encircles the neck. Otherwise the two forms are extremely similar in habitat, diet, size, proportions, general appearance, calls and behaviour.

NOISY ROOSTS

Lorikeets often roost in spectacularly large dormitories of several hundred individuals congregated in just a few trees. At sundown small groups rocket into these trees from all directions to be greeted by harsh screeches from those already at their perches. The birds squabble noisily over places and dash agitatedly about for some time before settling down for the night.

Scaly-breasted Lorikeet 23 cm

Lacking bright colours, the Scaly-breasted Lorikeet is best identified by its scaly green underparts.

The Scaly-breasted Lorikeet is very similar to the Rainbow Lorikeet except that it lacks its gaudy colouring and is found only in Australia. It is also very slightly smaller. The two birds are quite closely related, so much so that natural hybrids, although rare, are by no means unknown. The distribution of the Scaly-breasted Lorikeet extends from about Cooktown in Queensland to the vicinity of Wollongong in New South Wales, but its numbers decline north of about Maryborough and south of Sydney; it is very common in Brisbane. A small feral population near Melbourne is believed to have been founded by escaped cage-birds.

Habitat and Species Associates

The Scaly-breasted Lorikeet mainly inhabits coastal and nearby highland eucalypt forests and it travels long distances across the Great Dividing Range in search of nectar from flowering trees and shrubs. Occasionally it will stray into riverine woodlands further west or visit coastal heaths, paperbarks and other kinds of woodland. Scaly-breasted Lorikeets sometimes extend their diet to insects and fruit, and they may be troublesome in orchards.

Scaly-breasted Lorikeets quite often associate with Rainbow Lorikeets in mixed flocks but they are distinguished by their scaly green and yellow underparts, which are always obvious. Also their bright red underwings are conspicuous when the birds are in flight. The calls of the two species are very similar but those of the Scaly-breasted Lorikeet are just a little higher in pitch.

Varied Lorikeet

19 cm

A red cap and white 'goggles' are the main identifying features of the Varied Lorikeet.

In northern Australia's dry tropical woodlands the Varied Lorikeet is the most common of the lorikeet group, although it is rarely encountered east of the Gulf of Carpentaria. Birds usually occur in small parties rather than large flocks. Being strongly nomadic, they tend to be erratic in occurrence, appearing when local trees, especially bloodwoods, paperbarks and grevilleas, are in flower and then disappearing from the area for long periods of time. Feeding birds often utter a shrill chattering note but sometimes they forage quietly and at such times they are easily overlooked. In flight, however, flocks utter an almost constant excited thin screeching note.

Description and Breeding

The Varied Lorikeet is by far the smallest lorikeet in its range. Its bright red cap is unique among Australian lorikeets but its most obvious feature is its white 'goggles', an area of white feathers that surround each eye. Although males and females are similar, juvenile birds have greenish, not red, crowns.

As with many birds of the tropics, breeding can occur at any time of year but it reaches a peak during the dry season from about April to August. Varied Lorikeets usually select trees near water in which to nest. Sometimes they carpet the nest cavity with a few chewed leaves as well as woodchips obtained from modifying the entrance. They lay 2–4 eggs, which hatch in about 22 days; the chicks leave the nest about five weeks later.

What are Powder-downs?

*O*ne of the less obvious characteristics of parrots is their possession of powder-downs. Powder-downs are highly specialised types of down feathers. They are sparsely scattered throughout their plumage and are never moulted. They grow continuously and their tips constantly disintegrate to form a pale waxy powder. Parrots spread this powder throughout their plumage during their daily preening and grooming sessions. The result is a characteristic 'bloom' in the plumage but the function of powder-downs is not clearly understood.

Only a few birds possess powder-downs, including herons and one or two small groups of songbirds. In herons the powder-downs are generally supposed to assist in clearing fish slime from the plumage but there is no obvious correlation between powder-downs and other fish-eating birds.

Lorikeets spend much time preening to keep their plumage in good order.

Why are Parrots' Eggs White?

*B*irds lay eggs in a wide range of colours and patterns. Parrots' eggs, however, are white, unmarked and rounded, and those of one species are virtually indistinguishable from those of another except in size. Generally there is a trend for birds that build open nests to lay coloured eggs and for birds that nest in cavities to lay plain white ones. Colouring and patterning may disguise eggs efficiently from predators in the open but there is no advantage to coloration in the darkness of a tree hollow or burrow. Being white perhaps helps the incubating bird to find eggs more easily inside the gloom of a cavity. As to shape, round eggs would have a tendency to roll in the open so oval is more manageable but in the confines of a cavity this advantage is rendered redundant.

Galahs' eggs are round and white, differing from the eggs of all other cockatoos, lorikeets and parrots only in their size.

Choosing a Home

A Purple-crowned Lorikeet peers from its nest. Tree hollows make secure nests but they need to be defended constantly.

*B*irds in general use one or other of two devices for cradling and sheltering their eggs: they build a nest of grass or twigs, or they lay them in a hole in a tree. Numerous field studies have shown that tree cavities are safer and that chicks raised in tree cavities survive to fledge more often than comparable chicks reared in nests.

The downside is the 'rent' is much higher. A bird in a tree cavity must invest a great deal of its resources in defending its choice against the threat of eviction by others of its kind, as well as from a wide range of other woodland creatures seeking shelter from the elements. Moreover, the supply of tree cavities is always limited.

Parrots have several advantages over many other birds in this contest. Many species are big and aggressive enough to easily repel most trespassers. Their diet and feeding style is unusually efficient, so they can spare more time from foraging than many other birds. Also their strong pair bond means that the male is available to defend the site, leaving the female free to concentrate on child-rearing.

FOSSIL PARROTS

The oldest of all known birds, called *Archaeopteryx*, is about 140 million years old but parrots are very much more recent. The oldest known fossil that is indisputably a parrot is from France, a fragment of leg bone found in upper Oligocene deposits some 30 million years old. Australian fossil finds indicate that by about 20 million years ago there were cockatoos much like those living today.

Statistically, these Turquoise Parrot chicks are a little safer in their tree-hollow nest than they would be in a open nest of sticks.

Who are the 'Southern' Lorikeets?

The Musk Lorikeet is common in open forests and along timbered watercourses of the southeast.

*L*orikeets are essentially birds of the tropics but a group of three small species live mainly in southern Australia: these are the Musk, Purple-crowned and Little Lorikeets. Only about half the size of the familiar Rainbow Lorikeet, all three of these 'southern' lorikeets are strongly associated with flowering trees in eucalypt woodland. All three are similar in general appearance and behaviour, and all are mostly green with multicoloured faces.

As in other lorikeets, there are no significant differences in appearances between male and female or young and old birds. Working out their species identity from scattered glimpses through flowers and foliage in the top of a tree is not easy either but the colour of the underwings and details of the face pattern are the most important clues.

Musk Lorikeet

At about 22 cm long, the Musk Lorikeet is slightly larger than the other two 'southern' lorikeets. Strongly nomadic, it is widespread in southeastern Australia. Much more numerous in the south than in the north, it seldom wanders north of Brisbane. In Tasmania it is the only common lorikeet. Sometimes Musk Lorikeets occur together with Little Lorikeets in flowering trees and the two are easily confused despite the difference in size. The trick is to look for a patch of red extending behind the eye. Little Lorikeets also have red faces but the red lies almost wholly between the eye and the bill. Note also the Musk Lorikeet's red-tipped bill and green underwings.

Purple-crowned Lorikeet

About 16 cm long, the Purple-crowned Lorikeet occurs across southern Australia from the vicinity of Perth to the Mallacoota region of Victoria. However, it is absent from Tasmania and the Nullarbor Plain and rare east of Melbourne, although vagrants occasionally reach New South Wales and even Queensland. It often occurs on coastal heaths and in the west it is common in karri and jarrah forests. In southern cities such as Adelaide it is often common in suburban parks and gardens. The deep purple crown is distinctive but it also differs from Musk and Little Lorikeets in its red underwing coverts.

A deep purple cap is a distinctive feature of the Purple-crowned Lorikeet; the sexes are nearly identical.

Little Lorikeet

With a length of only 15 cm, half that of the Rainbow Lorikeet, the Little Lorikeet is the smallest of all Australian lorikeets. It is widespread across much of eastern Australia, from the vicinity of Cairns in Queensland to far western Victoria, and it once occurred in South Australia. It has also been recorded as a rare vagrant in Tasmania.

The Little Lorikeet sometimes joins other lorikeets at flowering trees, when it is usually best identified by its red face – it is important to note that the red does not extend behind the eye. If it is possible for you to see it, the red chin is also unique; Musk Lorikeets have green chins.

The Little Lorikeet is distinguished from other small lorikeets by red markings in front of its eyes.

FRANTIC FEEDERS

Small lorikeets can afford their frenetic activity. Research has shown that these small birds can obtain all of their daily food requirements in little more than two hours of feeding at a flowering gum tree, leaving plenty of energy to spare for widespread searching of other sources when the nectar supplies dry up.

THE GRASS PARROTS

What are Grass Parrots?

*W*hile most parrots live in trees and generally favour wooded areas, grass parrots are a distinctive group of small parrots that spend almost all of their time on the ground and live in open country. Here they feed on grass seeds and similar plants. The grass parrots or grass parakeets, as they are sometimes known, are confined to southern Australia.

Despite its uncharacteristic pastel pink and blue colour pattern, Bourke's Parrot is a typical grass parrot, inhabiting open country and feeding largely on the ground.

Most grass parrots are nomadic or undertake seasonal movements to some extent, and they include one of the very few strongly migratory parrots, the rare Orange-bellied Parrot. Their flight is characteristic, difficult to describe but quickly learnt: high, quick and easy, with a brief hesitation between each wing-beat. Grass parrots' calls are also distinctive, mostly variations of a sort of thin, silvery twitter. With the exception of the very different Bourke's Parrot, the plumage of grass parrots is mainly green or greenish and they usually have blue shoulders. In order to identify one from another, features of the face, forehead and shoulders are most useful.

A Rocky Spot to Nest

*T*he grass parrots include one of the very few Australian parrots that does not nest in a tree cavity. This is the Rock Parrot, which nests mainly on small offshore islands that are generally treeless. They lay their eggs in a sheltered depression on a ledge or in a crevice between boulders, usually well screened and hidden behind a curtain of vegetation. Breeding from August to December, they lay a clutch of 4–5 eggs which they incubate for 18 days. At first clad in white down, chicks gain their feathers and leave the nest at about 30 days, although they usually remain with their parents until the following spring.

The Rock Parrot is unusual in that it nests mainly in crevices between boulders on small offshore islands.

Are Parrots Territorial?

When young parrots first leave their parents, they usually gather in wandering flocks for the first year or two. At some point in this nomadic interlude they form pairs and that pair bond generally lasts for life. Resident species, such as many of the cockatoos, lay permanent claim to a nest cavity, which they use year after year and mark as theirs by gouging an area of the nearby trunk with claw and beak scratches to inform other cockatoos that the hole is taken.

Some nomadic or migratory species, such as the Swift Parrot on the other hand, must take what they can find wherever they are when the breeding season begins. Such parrots often nest in loose colonies with sometimes several cavities in a single tree being occupied.

In comparison with nomadic and migratory species, resident species are much more vigorous in ejecting trespassers from the vicinity of their nest cavity. Even so, how 'vicinity' is interpreted varies widely: while Galahs tolerate intruders of their own species anywhere beyond about 10 metres of their nest, to a Major Mitchell's Cockatoo 'nearby' means anything within several kilometres.

Like other cockatoos, the Short-billed Black-Cockatoo is territorial, defending its permanent nesting hollow from the threat of all trespassers.

SEALING THE BOND

Mated parrots are very affectionate with each other but their pair bond is also reinforced by a behaviour called courtship feeding, whereby a courting male offers his prospective mate an item of food. This ritual also becomes an integral part of their daily lives together. In the nesting season, while she is incubating the eggs, the female lives mainly on food brought to her by her mate.

Courtship feeding is a prominent feature and a permanent part of pair bonding.

Bourke's Parrot
19 cm

Bourke's Parrots normally drink only at night but on very hot days they may visit water frequently.

An inhabitant mainly of arid mulga scrub, Bourke's Parrot is one of the most desert-adapted of all the parrots and its distribution sprawls across the arid interior of the Australian continent, although it is mainly found south of the Tropic of Capricorn. In these remote areas it is reasonably common and may even have increased in numbers since about the 1950s when stock dams for watering cattle in the outback began to proliferate.

Uncharacteristic Colouring and Habits

The coloration of Bourke's Parrot is neither typical of the grass parrots nor indeed is it like that of any other parrot. Both males and females are easily identified by their pastel shades of pink, blue and brown.

Usually encountered in pairs or small parties, they are irregularly nomadic, sometimes remaining in a locality for several years before moving on. Like other small desert parrots, they come regularly to waterholes to drink but normally only during the hours of darkness. In other respects they resemble the quiet and unobtrusive behaviour of other grass parrots, spending much of their time on the ground, foraging on fallen seeds of grasses, herbs and shrubs. They are usually extremely tame and when disturbed often merely flutter up into a nearby bush to wait for the disturbance to pass.

Scarlet-chested Parrot
20 cm

The male Scarlet-chested Parrot (above) is easily distinguished from the female (right) by his striking red breast.

The beautiful male Scarlet-chested Parrot is easily identified by the splash of brilliant scarlet across its upper breast. Females lack this feature but are otherwise similar. Perhaps the most elusive of all the grass parrots, the Scarlet-chested Parrot is largely restricted to the most arid parts of the southern interior and is strongly nomadic. When it does occur at a particular locality, it is likely to do so in considerable numbers. It remains for a time to breed, then disappears, perhaps not to return to the area for several decades.

Localities where it has been reported extend from far western New South Wales to the vicinity of Kalgoorlie, Western Australia, and north approximately to Alice Springs.

MORE COMMON IN CAPTIVITY

Judging from the scarcity of reports, the Scarlet-chested Parrot may be one of Australia's rarest birds but a survey of aviculturists some years ago revealed that a total of at least 20,000 birds are held in captivity in Australia alone and that the species is also very popular among aviculturists overseas.

True Desert Dwellers

The Scarlet-chested Parrot is a true desert nomad and, more than perhaps any other parrot, it seems able to survive without water. Apparently always ready to breed at short notice, it seems able to detect temporarily good conditions from vast distances, arriving to nest quickly, then scattering again before conditions deteriorate. Australia has several bird species including, remarkably, a duck and a grebe that organise their lives in a similar fashion, although what clues they use to guide their movements remain entirely mysterious.

Blue-winged Parrot

20–21 cm

A pair of Blue-winged Parrots at their nest in an old weathered tree stump.

Aptly named, the male Blue-winged Parrot is best identified by the large expanse of deep blue in its wings: this far exceeds the blue shoulder patches of other grass parrots. Females and young are confusingly similar to females of several other small grass parrots so they are best identified by the company they keep. The situation is, however, often complicated by the fact that Blue-winged Parrots sometimes form mixed flocks with Elegant Parrots in winter.

Seasonal Movements

Less fussy about its habitat requirements than most other grass parrots, the Blue-winged Parrot nests in spring and summer in open woodland and heath in Tasmania (including many of the islands in Bass Strait), Victoria and southeastern South Australia. Here it is usually in pairs or small parties. In autumn much of the population moves northward to spend the winter on the vast flat saltbush and bluebush plains of far western New South Wales and northeastern South Australia where it sometimes congregates in large flocks.

The Blue-winged Parrot is generally common and widespread. Like other grass parrots, it forages inconspicuously on the ground, feeding mainly on fallen seeds.

KEEPING IN TOUCH

In summer grass parrots are usually seen in pairs or family parties but flocks of up to perhaps 100 birds or so often congregate in winter. When flying they keep in touch with one another with abrupt, trisyllabic 'tsit-tsit-tsit' contact calls that vary only slightly between species.

Elegant Parrot

22 cm

Resplendent in its yellow-green plumage, an Elegant Parrot heads for its nest.

The Elegant Parrot is reasonably common in southeastern Australia, from the extreme southwestern corner of New South Wales to Kangaroo Island and the Mount Lofty Ranges in South Australia. It also occurs in southwestern Western Australia from about Shark Bay to Esperance.

Often confused with the Blue-winged Parrot when in mixed flocks during winter, the Elegant Parrot can be distinguished by its wings. These are distinctly two-toned deep blue and light blue rather than featuring the much more extensive uniformly deep blue wing patches of the Blue-winged Parrot.

A Parrot of Edges and Clearings

Although it can also be found in open environments, such as coastal sand dunes or interior saltbush plains, the Elegant Parrot shows a special fondness for forest edges and clearings. In fact, those mosaic situations that commonly occur when woodlands are cleared for pasture, leaving only remnants or perhaps woodlots, result in a habitat well suited to the Elegant Parrot and flocks often visit improved pastures to feed on the seeds of introduced grasses, such as clover and paspalum.

> **HIGH FLIERS**
> Grass parrots habitually fly high. On the western plains, for example, it is not unusual to see parties of Blue-winged Parrots flying from horizon to horizon at considerable height, barely visible to the naked eye with only their contact calls drifting down to betray their identity.

Which Parrot Made a Remarkable Comeback?

*O*nce widespread in south-eastern Australia, populations of Turquoise Parrots suffered a devastating collapse around the turn of the century, a decline so severe that in 1920 they were described by at least one contemporary researcher as 'possibly extinct in New South Wales and Victoria'. However, since the 1940s there has been a vigorous recovery and it is now reasonably common in many parts of eastern New South Wales. The reasons for this parrot's decline and its subsequent recovery remain unknown.

Grass, rock, timber and water are the main elements of the Turquoise Parrot's rigid habitat requirements.

What Parrot Pulls a Crowd ?

The Orange-bellied Parrot nests only on Tasmania's remote western shore.

*T*he rare Orange-bellied Parrot pulls a big crowd. With a total population estimated at less than 400 individuals, it is one of the most seriously endangered species in Australia. At its summer breeding ground in the remote southwest of Tasmania it is impractical to count these birds but in its mainland winter habitat it is more visible. Along the Victorian coastline, especially on the saltmarshes fringing Port Phillip Bay, the birds are counted each year by an enthusiastic band of volunteers. Every winter since 1978, these volunteers have enrolled for a coordinated census of the birds to assess their population trends. Such time-consuming and laborious population monitoring is a vital part of any endangered species management project. In assessing management strategies, it is important to know if numbers are rising or falling.

Why are Native Grasses Important?

Over millennia the grass parrots have reached a point of equilibrium with their major source of food: native grasses. There are a wide range of native grasses and these seed at different times of year according to climatic conditions. The pattern in which these grasses produce seed provides the parrots with a year-round source of food, or rather it did.

The Mulga Parrot depends on a rich community of native grasses to provide it with year-round sustenance.

This delicate balance has been profoundly disrupted by changes in land use arising from European settlement. Increases in grazing livestock, the introduction of 'improved' or exotic grasses, changes in the use of fire, and habitat degradation by rabbits and other introduced animals have all contributed to this shift. These changes are having serious effects on many Australian parrots, including the Turquoise Parrot, and it is believed that this disruption of the seeding cycles of native grasses may in fact have exterminated the Paradise Parrot.

SMUGGLING

In Australia, all export of native birds is illegal, yet trapping of wild Australian parrots does occur and it has had a profound effect on many populations. Most individuals smuggled out of the country die of stress in transit.

Enormous ingenuity is used by parrot smugglers to evade detection by customs and wildlife authorities but appalling wastage is one characteristic all methods have in common — probably only two in ten parrots will survive the transit to foreign markets.

Orange-bellied Parrot

20–21 cm

A bright orange patch on the belly is a prominent but variable feature of the Orange-bellied Parrot.

With a total world population of less than 400 individuals, the Orange-bellied Parrot is one of Australia's rarest and most seriously endangered birds and it is one of our very few strongly migratory parrots. It breeds only in swamps, moors and fens in remote parts of western Tasmania, seldom more than about 60 km from the coast. In autumn it migrates across Bass Strait to spend the winter along the Victorian coast. Today the bulk of the population is found on samphire flats, sand dunes and paddocks around Port Phillip Bay but once it ranged westward to the Coorong in South Australia.

Description

The orange patch on its belly is variable and difficult to see, but the Orange-bellied Parrot differs most obviously from other grass parrots by the fact that the overall colour impression is distinctly bright grass green, whereas other grass parrots appear yellowish, olive or even khaki. There is little difference between the sexes.

GOING BY VOICE

While with practice it is not hard to tell one grass parrot species from another by voice, it is also true that all have common qualities very different from other parrots. Grass parrot calls are thin, high-pitched, sharp and often have a twittering or tinkling quality.

Habits and Call

The Orange-bellied Parrot usually occurs in small flocks in winter, when it spends almost all of its time on the ground; even when not feeding, it is likely to be found sheltering quietly from sun or wind beneath a bush or grass tussock. It eats mainly the seeds of samphire and similar plants but birds have also been seen eating seaweed. Its alarm call, 'chitter-chitter', has a distinctive dry, buzzing quality.

The overall khaki hue of the Rock Parrot is its distinctive identifying feature.

Rock Parrot   22 cm

A typical Rock Parrot lives out its entire life within the sound of the ocean surf and it is unusual to find one more than a few kilometres from the coast. It is a bird of sand dunes, tidal flats and rocky off-shore islands all along the southern coast of Australia from about Kingston to Ceduna in South Australia and from Cape Arid to Geraldton in Western Australia, including many outlying islands such as the Recherche Archipelago.

The Rock Parrot is partly migratory in that most pairs breed on small offshore stacks and islets and then move to adjacent mainland coasts to spend the winter. Although locally common, its population has suffered a marked decline in the east over recent decades. It could once be found at several localities around Adelaide but now an observer will probably need to go much farther west to be sure of encountering it.

Male Turquoise Parrots have distinctive deep reddish shoulder patches.

Turquoise Parrot   20 cm

The Turquoise Parrot is most numerous where rocky mountain-sides, grassy glades and open woodlands come together. The Warrumbungles and the Capertee Valley in New South Wales are good examples of this kind of country. It is widespread from the Victorian high country, along the Great Dividing Range, especially along the western slopes, northwards to around Maryborough in Queensland but its distribution tends to be patchy because large stretches of land interrupt its most suitable habitat.

Turquoise Parrots like to forage in long grass, preferring the dappled shade of over-hanging trees to open sunny patches. Like other grass parrots they are tame, quiet and inconspicuous in their behaviour. They are easily overlooked and usually not seen until they fly up suddenly, almost underfoot, revealing bright yellow outer tail feathers. Adult males bear an obvious patch of deep red on the shoulders but females and young birds are difficult to distinguish from other grass parrots, although confusion is unlikely since other grass parrots seldom stray into the kind of country favoured by Turquoise Parrots.

THE ROSELLAS

Crimson Rosella

36 cm

Adult Crimson Rosellas have vivid hues of rich crimson and blue but immature birds are mainly dull green.

Visit any campground or picnic spot in the forest almost anywhere in coastal eastern and southeastern Australia or the associated highlands and snow country and this is likely to be the first parrot you will notice. Crimson Rosellas are usually abundant in tall forest and easily seen in flocks or small parties foraging along roadsides and in grassy clearings. In many places the birds come to beg for handouts and they are often so tame they can be fed by hand.

The Crimson Rosella occurs all along the Great Dividing Range and its associated highlands southward from the Atherton Tableland in far northern Queensland. Where woodlands are more open it tends to be replaced by the closely related Eastern Rosella. The Crimson Rosella has also been introduced to New Zealand and Norfolk Island.

ROSELLA VOICES

Crimson Rosellas have a range of calls but three calls are especially distinctive. When alarmed or disturbed, they utter a shrill shrieking note; when perched and self-absorbed they make soft and mellow piping whistles; and their distinctive contact call, normally uttered in flight, is a brisk 'cuss-ik, cuss-ik'.

Description

Adult males and females are nearly identical, both having red bodies and blue cheeks, but the Crimson Rosella is one of the few Australian parrots with a distinctive juvenile plumage: young Crimson Rosellas are mainly green rather than red, a fact that has confused many a birdwatcher. It takes several years to attain the crimson plumage and the young birds, still in their green plumage, often form roving bands that contain no adults. When moulting into their adult plumage, Crimson Rosellas are green with irregular red patches.

Green Rosella

37 cm

Confined to Tasmania, the Green Rosella is a common bird of forests, parks and gardens.

The Green Rosella is very common in most wooded habitats throughout Tasmania and the islands of Bass Strait. It is a very close relative of the Crimson Rosella and the two species are very similar in size, calls, general behaviour and lifestyle. The Crimson Rosella does not occur in Tasmania at all and the two rosellas are often treated as different forms of the same species.

Description and Habits

Adult Green Rosellas look in fact very like the juveniles of the mainland Crimson Rosellas. The head and underparts are deep yellow except for blue cheeks and a broad band of red across the forehead. The tail and back are blackish olive and the rump is bright olive.

Although adult Green Rosellas often form small parties in winter when they may leave mountainous regions in search of milder conditions at lower altitudes, they are mainly sedentary. Juveniles, on the other hand, form nomadic flocks of 20 birds or so. Like other rosellas, seeds gathered on the ground constitute the chief food but Green Rosellas are also particularly fond of the berries of the introduced hawthorn, a prominent plant along Tasmanian roadsides. They will also eat cultivated fruit of various kinds and can sometimes be troublesome in orchards.

Why are Parrots so Brightly Coloured?

*T*he quick answer is because they can afford to be. All animals confront two opposing imperatives: they must be conspicuous to their mates while remaining hidden from their predators. There are no solutions to this contradiction and every position is a compromise.

In general, birds that are large have less to fear from predators than those that are small and birds that flock have less to fear from predators than solitary birds because there are more eyes to spot danger. Parrots have an advantage in this respect which makes them suitable contenders for some striking apparel in the plumage line.

Also, where many related species occur together, as in parrots, it becomes particularly important that each species be promptly recognised for what it is: if there is confusion among the sexes, this will inevitably lead to missing out in the mating stakes. Conspicuous markings and distinc-

The vibrant Red-winged Parrot is one of Australia's most brightly coloured parrots.

tive colours are therefore an advantage when it comes to propagating the species. So, taking all factors into account, parrots do not need to fear predators but they do need to be concerned about mixing themselves up, so their particular compromise leans towards the flamboyant rather than the unobtrusive.

Parrots that Glow in the Dark

Some parrots' brightest feathers are visible only under ultraviolet light, like those of these Eastern Rosellas.

*H*uman eyes see three colours: red, blue and green, and all other visible colours result from combinations of these. Some birds, notably pigeons and hummingbirds, are known to see four colours: their eyes are sensitive also to ultraviolet light. Although little is known at present about what birds do with this enhanced capability, perhaps there is more than a hint involved in a recent discovery concerning the plumage of parrots, which apparently glow in the dark.

Ultraviolet 'colours' become visible to human eyes if you shine an ultraviolet light on them, which makes them glow. Not too long ago a museum ornithologist took a notion to turn out the lights and shine an ultraviolet light on his parrot specimens and found that they fluoresced strongly. He discovered that both the Sulphur-crested Cockatoo's crest and the Budgerigar's forehead glows strongly in the dark, as does the Eastern Rosella's back. These are parts used prominently in courtship, so there is a strong suggestion that the fluorescent pigments are involved somehow in mating but so far it is not even known for certain whether parrot eyes are sensitive to ultraviolet frequencies.

Where do Parrots' Bright Colours Come From?

Some bright colours result from the microscopic structure of feathers.

*T*he colours of feathers arise from two chief causes. Many colours are formed from pigments — chemical substances that produce colour in exactly the same way as paints and the dyes in clothing. Most shades of brown, yellow and red in a bird's feathers arise in this way, and carotenes — the same family of pigments that make carrots red and the chemical foundation of vitamin A — are the chief sources. Blacks result from melanin, the same pigment that makes human skin dark.

Other colours are structural; they cannot be bleached out or removed by any chemical treatment. Blues, for example, are formed by the same mechanism that makes the sky look blue, the microscopic structure of the feather absorbing some wavelengths of light and reflecting others. There are no blue pigments among birds. Shades of green result from a combination of the two effects: yellow pigment combines with structural blue to yield green.

Sulphur-crested Cockatoos use their mobile crests to convey a variety of moods and feelings.

FAMILY CRESTS

Bright colours work well as 'signals' to other birds at a distance but movable crests are even better for very close work among birds that spend a great deal of their time together, such as cockatoos. A cockatoo can tell its mate a great deal about its mood, or signal excitement or interest, or even warn of danger, simply by the angle to which it raises its crest.

A brightly coloured Eastern Rosella.

Eastern Rosella 28–30 cm

The Eastern Rosella is common in open woodlands across much of the southeast, including Tasmania. Its most striking features include a bright red head and breast with contrasting white cheek patches and a yellow belly and yellow edges to the feathers of its back. One of its most useful identification features is the bright apple green rump, a feature that is very obvious when these birds take to the air.

Eastern Rosellas are active and conspicuous except when feeding; then they are easily overlooked. They eat mainly seeds which they gather from the ground but their diets also include insects, nectar, fruit, nuts, flowers and buds. Their calls include mellow piping notes uttered when perched, a contact call usually given in flight, alarm screeches and soft conversational chattering notes. Rosellas are usually encountered in pairs or small parties but they may band together in larger flocks in winter.

An adult Pale-headed Rosella.

Pale-headed Rosella 30 cm

The Pale-headed Rosella ranges from extreme northeastern New South Wales northward to Cape York Peninsula and westward approximately to Charleville, Blackall and Croydon in Queensland. Although chiefly a bird of lowland savanna woodlands, it also occurs in riverine woodlands, coastal heaths and a variety of other lightly timbered habitats.

Its plumage pattern is distinctive: a light yellow head, white cheek patches, pale blue underparts and red undertail coverts. The population on Cape York Peninsula is somewhat paler than birds from the south with the cheek patches suffused with pale blue and a light yellow band across the upper breast.

Despite their obvious plumage differences, the Pale-headed and Eastern Rosellas are very closely related and they interbreed with some frequency where their ranges come together along the border between Queensland and New South Wales. Calls, diet, behaviour and nesting regimes are also similar. Interbreeding is so widespread, in fact, that many researchers prefer to regard the Eastern Rosella and Pale-headed Rosella as local forms of a single species which is often named the White-cheeked Rosella.

Northern Rosellas coming in to drink.

Northern Rosella   28cm

The Northern Rosella is the Top End representative of the rosellas, with a distribution that includes the Kimberley and the northern part of the Northern Territory, south to around Katherine and east to the head of the Gulf of Carpentaria. Its most obvious plumage characteristic is its mainly black head, with white cheek patches and dusky yellow underparts.

It inhabits most kinds of open savanna woodland and associated habitats. Although resembling its close relatives, the Pale-headed Rosella and the Eastern Rosella, in almost every aspect of lifestyle and behaviour, the Northern Rosella seems very much less numerous and more elusive than its southern and eastern relatives.

A Western Rosella alighting at its nest hollow.

WHAT'S IN A NAME?
The name rosella originates from what is now the suburb of Rose Hill, which lies on one of the oldest routes linking Parramatta and Sydney. In the late 1700s, travellers noted the Eastern Rosella's abundance at Rose Hill and called the birds 'Rose Hill Parrots', a name that ultimately became shortened to 'rosella'.

Western Rosella   26 cm

This rosella has a restricted distribution in the far southwestern corner of Western Australia, south and west of a line drawn between approximately Moora and Dundas. It inhabits most kinds of timbered country, including coastal heath, croplands, orchards and even urban parks and gardens. Usually encountered in pairs or family parties, it is much less inclined to form large flocks than other rosellas and it tends to feed more on the ground and less in the trees than rosellas of the eastern States.

The Western Rosella is easily the smallest of the rosellas, with a slimmer, more elegant build than the others. It is also noticeably quieter and more easily overlooked. The head and underparts are bright red and the cheek patches are yellow. Adult male and female rosellas usually look similar but Western Rosellas are easily distinguished as females are much duller than males.

Who are the Rosellas?

Distinctive features of all the rosellas are their coloured cheek-patches and scaly backs.

*T*he two most obvious distinguishing characteristics of the rosellas are features of pattern, not colour: scalloped backs and coloured cheek patches. In all rosellas the back is black, each feather broadly rimmed with some contrasting colour to produce a scalloped effect, and there is a large patch of contrasting colour on the face. The colour may be green, red, white, yellow or blue according to species but these two features of pattern are common to all rosellas.

The rosellas of eastern Australia fall into two main groups: those with blue cheek patches (the Crimson Rosella and its relatives) and those with white cheek patches (the Eastern Rosella and its relatives). All of the rosella forms are very closely related; the difficulty lies in deciding just how close that relationship is. Some researchers prefer to regard them all as forming just two species, the White-cheeked Rosella and the Blue-cheeked Rosella.

Are any Parrots Pests?

*S*everal parrots, notably the Crimson Rosella and the Australian King-Parrot in the east and the Red-capped Parrot in the west, occasionally cause severe damage in orchards and, until handling methods were changed in recent years, Galahs caused widespread spoilage to stored grain but hardly any Australian parrots rank as serious or widespread agricultural pests. A conspicuous exception is the Long-billed Corella; in this case wildlife managers are confronted with the unusual challenge of an endangered bird causing serious agricultural damage. The Long-billed Corella has a severely restricted distribution and its total population is very small. Nevertheless, it is sometimes locally very abundant and large flocks can ruin cereal crops in its core distribution area of western Victoria.

Although not a serious pest, the Australian King-Parrot may cause severe damage to orchard crops.

Do Sibling Parrots Hatch Together?

Most parrots lay an egg every two days, which means it takes a little over a week to produce a typical clutch of four. Since the embryo starts growing only when incubation begins, important consequences arise from whether the female begins incubation with the first egg or waits till the clutch is complete. Eastern Rosellas wait till the last egg is laid, which means all the eggs hatch together. Her chicks are all equal in size and she can keep her brood together more easily even after they leave the nest. Desert nomads like the Budgerigar, on the other hand, often do things

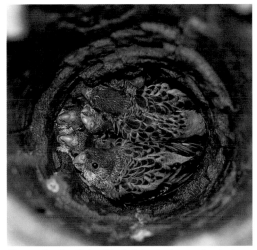

Eastern Rosella chicks differ little in size because incubation does not commence until the clutch is complete.

differently. Incubation may begin with the first or second egg, which means the clutch hatches at staggered intervals. The mother thus has chicks of all sizes to deal with in the nest but there are important advantages. If conditions remain good, she can probably raise all her chicks but if the food supply should suddenly fail then perhaps at least the largest chick can be reared and the nesting attempt need not be a total failure.

Australian ringnecks resemble rosellas; both have the tendency to differ strikingly in details of plumage according to region.

ROSELLAS AND RINGNECKS

Rosellas and ringnecks may look very different in plumage but they are extremely similar in all other respects. Rosellas are essentially birds of coastal and near-coastal woodlands, whereas their cousins, the ringnecks, occupy the arid interior. Both groups are made up of several geographically separated forms and subspecies.

Who are the Ringnecks?

*A*cross the arid interior of Australia live several forms of parrot that are very like the rosellas in size and general appearance but which feature a broad band of yellow across their nape, hence their common name, ringnecks. These are among the commonest and most conspicuous Australian parrots in most kinds of inland open wooded country. Quite at home in the narrow belt of timber that borders many outback roads, they are often seen by motorists.

The Twenty-eight Parrot was once regarded as a separate species of ringneck; now all forms are seen as a single variable species.

The Four Different Forms

The ringnecks were once regarded as four distinct species: the Twenty-eight Parrot, the Port Lincoln Parrot, the Mallee Ringneck and the Cloncurry Parrot. Today all forms are usually regarded as making up a single variable species and all of them interbreed wherever they come together. The four forms have clearly been separated at some time in the past but not for long enough to have evolved specifically distinct features.

There is a trend for ringnecks to become larger, darker and more richly coloured from east to west and from north to south.

The most richly coloured form, the Twenty-eight Parrot, has a black head, deep green breast and a band of red across the forehead. It occurs south and west of the wheatbelt in Western Australia. Inland from the wheatbelt lives another form, the Port Lincoln Ringneck, which is very similar except that it usually lacks the red forehead band and its belly is bright yellow instead of green.

A plain black head, mostly lacking red markings, is the most distinctive feature of the Port Lincoln Ringneck, the mid-western form of the widespread ringnecks.

The Mallee Ringneck is common in dry woodlands across the eastern interior.

Much of the eastern interior is occupied by the Mallee Ringneck, which differs most obviously in having a green, not black, head. Its underparts are green and it has a narrow band of red across the forehead. Yet another form, smaller and paler, inhabits open woodlands in the vicinity of Mount Isa and Cloncurry in inland northern Queensland: this is the so-called Cloncurry Parrot.

Shared Characteristics

All four forms are nearly identical in their diet, behaviour and nesting habits. They feed on a wide range of buds, flowers, seeds and other parts of plants, gathered both on the ground and in trees. Like other inland parrots, they drink at least daily, roost together in trees at night and usually spend several hours during the heat of the day in a 'siesta' period spent quietly perched in shady trees. Ringnecks live mostly in family parties and they are less inclined than many other parrots to form large flocks, even in winter. The breeding season is very variable in both timing and duration: in drought years the birds may not breed at all, whereas in good seasons they may raise two broods in quick succession.

URBAN RINGNECKS

Occasionally 'black-headed' ringnecks make an appearance in the centre of eastern cities, such as Sydney, where originally no form ever occurred. These local populations have been founded by escaped cage-birds, often Port Lincoln or Twenty-eight Parrots.

OFFSHORE PARROTS

Eclectus Parrot

42 cm

The male Eclectus Parrot (above) is so strikingly different from his mate (right) that the two sexes were once considered different species.

The Eclectus Parrot ranges from eastern Indonesia through New Guinea to the Solomon Islands but in Australia it occurs only on Cape York Peninsula, from about the McIllwraith Range northwards. Like the smaller Red-cheeked Parrot, it flies high and calls freely, so it is conspicuous in flight but often hard to see when feeding in the canopy. Although it is largely confined to rainforest, it often visits fruiting trees in other kinds of forest and woodland.

One of the most striking features of the Eclectus Parrot is the great difference in the male and female plumages: males are mainly bright emerald green but females are mostly deep red, with a bright blue belly. Although the bill is dull black in both sexes, in males it bears a patch of coral pink.

Habits, Flight and Voice

Eclectus Parrots very seldom visit the ground. They are usually encountered in small parties feeding in trees flying between food sources but up to 80 birds or more may congregate at roosting trees. They are noisy birds, uttering a variety of loud, strident, screeching calls. Their flight is distinctive: direct, not especially swift and often interrupted by periods of gliding, the wings never rising above the horizontal plane.

> **TELLING THE DIFFERENCE**
> So different is the plumage of the male Eclectus Parrot from that of his female counterpart that for nearly a century after these birds were discovered in 1776 the two were believed to be different species.

Red-cheeked Parrot 22 cm

The Red-cheeked Parrot is confined to the rainforests of New Guinea and Cape York.

Although very much smaller, the silhouette of the Red-cheeked Parrot in flight greatly resembles that of the Eclectus Parrot. Indeed both species look bulky in flight and have short, blunt tails and broad wings. Both are also very much birds of the treetops, frequently flying high and seldom visiting the ground. In Australia, both, too, are confined to the rainforests of Cape York Peninsula.

Plumage
The plumage of Red-cheeked Parrots is mainly bright green but adult females have dull brown heads and adult males have a deep violet crown and red cheeks. Immature males have green heads and take at least two years to reach adult plumage.

Habitat and Habits
Red-cheeked Parrots are noisy, conspicuous birds when they fly high above the forest canopy with shallow, hurried wingbeats but they can be very difficult to see when feeding in the treetops. The birds eat a wide range of seeds, nuts and fruits. Although most common in rainforest, they often also forage in mangrove swamps and open woodlands. They are usually encountered in pairs or small parties but gather at dusk in communal roosts. The most common call is a loud 'klee...klee...klee' with a distinctive brisk, strident, metallic quality.

New Guinean Animals Marooned in Australia

New Guinea is now separated from Australia by Torres Strait but it was not always so. The seas of Torres Strait and the adjacent Arafura Sea to the west are extremely shallow and until as recently as 8,000 years ago dry land connected the two landmasses. Much of the region now under the sea was then one vast tropical rainforest, extending south part way down what is now Cape York Peninsula. Its wide-

Narrow straits that separate Cape York (above) from New Guinea were once linked by a vast track of rainforested land.

spread inhabitants included the Eclectus Parrot and the Red-cheeked Parrot.

As the Earth emerged from the last Ice Age, warmer climate began melting the polar ice caps and sea levels around the world rose accordingly. Ultimately the sea breached Torres Strait, cutting off and marooning such birds on what is now Australia from contact with their relatives on New Guinea. These two parrots are not the only essentially New Guinean animals provided in this way with a toehold in the very northern tip of Australia. Among birds the list includes the Trumpet Manucode and the Fawn-breasted Bowerbird and among mammals is the Common Spotted Cuscus.

Are New Zealand's Parrots Different?

Not all Australasian parrots occur in Australia or New Guinea, and several are confined to New Zealand. Among these is a group often known as

The Kaka is a typical member of New Zealand's small but very distinctive cluster of native parrot species.

kakarikis. These parakeets somewhat resemble a small rosella but are mainly green, with short, pointed tails. They have representatives on many offshore islands, among them a dull green parrot confined to the remote Auckland Islands, where it fossicks for seeds among the penguin colonies. New Zealand is also the headquarters of a group that includes the Kaka and the Kea, which is famous among tourists for its playful antics around the alpine ski slopes of the South Island.

Both of these characteristically New Zealand groups have (or had) members on Australian soil, although just barely. At the time of its discovery, Norfolk Island had its own endemic species of kaka; this, however, was very quickly exterminated. Similarly, the kakarikis had a representative, the Red-crowned Parakeet, on Macquarie, Lord Howe and Norfolk Islands. Like the Norfolk Island Kaka, it was soon exterminated on both Macquarie and Lord Howe Islands but it still survives on Norfolk Island.

Most knowledge of the extinct Norfolk Island Kaka is conveyed by this painting and one or two specimens.

Do Parrots Breed in Groups?

*A*ustralia has long been notable as the home of a remarkable number of species of birds that nest in groups — not simply in pairs. A group of Laughing Kookaburras, for example, share all nesting duties among themselves, cooperating to incubate, brood, rear and defend a single clutch of eggs laid by the oldest female in the group.

Until recently it was believed that such communal breeders did not include any Australian parrots but it now seems that the Eclectus Parrot may be an exception. In Australia the Eclectus Parrot nests only in the remote rainforests near the tip of Cape York Peninsula. Thorough studies of its life history have barely begun but several nests under careful scrutiny have been visited by adult parrots other than the owners and it seems highly likely that the Eclectus Parrot will prove to be a communal nester.

LITTLE DIGGERS
The Double-eyed Figparrot and the Red-cheeked Parrot nest in tree cavities like most other species of parrots but they are unique among the Australian parrots in one respect: they dig the cavities themselves. Other parrots often carry out renovations to their homes, especially around the entrance, but these are always merely modifications to an existing natural cavity.

The Eclectus Parrot is a possible contender for Australia's only communal breeder among parrots.

Double-eyed Figparrot   13 cm

The Double-eyed Figparrot is widespread in New Guinea and it occurs in Australia in three separate populations, one in each of the major rainforest blocks along the east coast: roughly from Grafton to Maryborough, Cardwell to Cooktown and towards the tip of Cape York. The southern population, often called Cox's Figparrot, is rarely seen and seriously endangered but the two northern populations remain common. The three differ in the detailed arrangement of patches of red and blue on the head.

At first glance these parrots might be mistaken for small lorikeets, especially when flying overhead in groups. Like lorikeets, their plumage is mostly green and their calls are a thin and intense 'zeet, zeet'. However, they are much tubbier in build, shorter tailed and smaller than any lorikeet. In fact, the Double-eyed Figparrot is Australia's smallest parrot.

True to its name, the Doubled-eyed Figparrot lives on a diet consisting almost entirely of several species of native figs.

Diet, Habits and Nesting

The birds call freely in flight but they are usually rather quiet and unobtrusive when feeding. They prefer figs but will also eat other rainforest fruits and may visit flowering trees for nectar. They are mainly confined to rainforests but occasionally visit more open woodlands and mangroves. Double-eyed Figparrots are usually encountered in pairs or small parties but up to 200 or so may congregate in communal roosts at night.

Very few nesting details are known but a common nesting site is a hole dug out mainly by the female in a rotten trunk or the stub of a rainforest tree. It seems that the female carries out most of the incubation and feeding of the chicks, although the male may assist with feeding the brood as they get older.

Red-crowned Parakeet   23 cm

Essentially a New Zealand species, the Red-crowned Parakeet also inhabits Australia's Norfolk Island.

In Australia the Red-crowned Parakeet occurs only on Norfolk Island off the east coast of the mainland. It once lived on Lord Howe Island and on remote subantarctic Macquarie Island. It is also widely distributed in New Zealand and New Caledonia.

Resembling the Crimson Rosella in much of its behaviour and lifestyle, the Red-crowned Parakeet is entirely green in plumage except for a red patch on the crown and ear coverts. It feeds mainly in trees, on a wide range of native and introduced fruits, berries, buds and seeds and occasionally forages on the ground. It is dependent on native forest, which means that individuals are effectively restricted to the slopes of Mount Pitt in the northern part of Norfolk Island. Although it is rarely seen, its call is unmistakable: a rapid, drawn out 'kek-kek-kek-kek'.

A Bleak Future

The Macquarie and Lord Howe Island populations quickly fell victim to the depredations of introduced rats and feral cats, and the Norfolk Island population may well follow them into oblivion: there are probably less than 30 birds in the entire population. However a vigorous captive-breeding program is now showing encouraging signs of reversing this trend.

MISSING RELATIVE

On Captain Cook's voyage across the Pacific in 1773 he called at the Society Islands, which are near Tahiti. Here he obtained two specimens of the so-called Society Parakeet, a close relative of the Red-crowned Parakeet. This species of parrot must have become extinct almost immediately afterwards as no other specimens have ever been recorded.

Other Parrots

What are 'Typical' Parrots?

Lacking an obvious crest and largely shunning nectar, the ringnecks are considered 'typical' or 'true' parrots.

*I*t is not easy to define 'typical' parrots except in terms of what is left after the lorikeets and cockatoos have been removed. The cockatoos have erectile crests and lorikeets feed almost entirely on nectar but most other features are common to all members of the group. Both lorikeets and cockatoos are almost entirely confined to Australasia but the 'typical' parrots occur almost everywhere in the tropics and many temperate regions as well, especially in the Southern Hemisphere.

Do Other Continents have Parrots ?

*A*ustralia is exceptionally well endowed with parrots but several South American countries — Brazil and Colombia, for example — are valid contenders for Australia's title of 'land of parrots'. The rainforests of Amazonia are especially notable for their several species of spectacularly large and colourful macaws. The macaws are even longer than Australian black-cockatoos, although they are not so heavily built.

Africa comes third in the parrot diversity stakes. It is home to the lovebirds — worldwide these parrots are popular as domestic pets, nearly as much so as Australian Budgerigars and Cockatiels. Africa is also the home of the Grey Parrot, famous among all parrots for being by far the most accomplished mimic of the human voice.

Clad in mainly vibrant red, the Scarlet Macaw is one of South America's numerous parrot species.

Stories of Talking Parrots

*A*lthough no species occurs naturally in Europe, parrots were well known to the ancient Greeks and Romans who were fascinated by their ability to mimic human speech. In ancient Greece, Aristotle's writings contain descriptions of parrots which were almost certainly based on specimens sent back to Europe by Alexander the Great during his expedition into India. Among the aristocracy of ancient Rome, talking parrots were an envied status symbol.

For centuries, talking parrots have featured in literature of all kinds. They are mentioned in at least three of Shakespeare's plays. Robinson Crusoe had a talking parrot, as did Peter Pan's arch foe, Captain Hook. In nineteenth-century adventure yarns, no manifestation of a pirate chief was complete without his talking parrot.

Do Parrots have Courtship Displays?

*T*hey do but these are usually much less spectacular than those of some other birds, such as the birds of paradise. Because most Australian parrots form pair bonds that last for life there is little need for elaborate courtship displays and most of these are low-key affairs directed more at maintaining the pair bond rather than initiating it.

The mating displays of the Superb Parrot, for example, are reasonably typical of the group, although a little more dramatic than most. As a prelude to mating, the male Superb Parrot flies around his 'wife' several times, lands in front of her and vigorously bows and bobs his head. He sleeks his body plumage, raises the feathers of his face and crown, and scuttles to and fro along his perch. His eyes are strongly dilated and he chatters excitedly. She finally invites him to mount her by crouching low on her perch, partly spreading her wings, and persuading him to feed her with soft begging calls. Such mating displays are confined to early in the breeding season but other rituals may continue into the nesting season.

Like most parrots, Turquoise Parrots live close to their mates and have little need for spectacular courtship displays.

Australian King-Parrot

41–43 cm

The colourful Australian King-Parrot is common and widespread in the forests of eastern Australia.

Australian King-Parrots favour the tall, dense, high-rainfall forests of eastern and southeastern Australia, roughly from Cooktown to Melbourne. The birds come readily to garden feeders in well-wooded suburbs but on the whole they are much shyer than other forest parrots. King-Parrots and Crimson Rosellas often occur together in the same habitats and they are easily confused — both are roughly the same size and shape, and mainly red below. The male King-Parrot is a striking-looking parrot. Sleek and resplendent, his pillar-box red head and underparts contrast sharply with his striking forest green back and upperwings plumage. Except for a light green shoulder stripe, this deep and brilliant colouring is unadulterated by other tones, shading or patterning. Females resemble males but they have dull green heads.

Movements and Foraging

King-Parrots are mainly sedentary or at least they are only nomadic within a quite small area. They congregate at communal roosts at dusk but scatter in pairs or small groups to forage in the early morning. They seldom form large flocks. King-Parrots are reluctant to feed on the ground. More usually they forage in trees and shrubs for a wide range of buds, berries, nuts and seeds; sometimes they cause damage in orchards and to other crops.

Red-winged Parrot

31–33 cm

Easily identified by its red wing patches, this parrot inhabits the drier woodlands of eastern Australia.

Although much smaller, the Red-winged Parrot is a sort of arid-land version of the Australian King-Parrot and the two species have broadly similar diets and feeding behaviour. The typical image of Red-winged Parrots is of a small group threading its way swiftly through the trees along some tropical dry-country riverbed. From this distance, they are most easily identified by their deep, wavering, oddly hesitant wingbeats and metallic 'krillik, krillik' calls.

Distribution, Habits and Description

The Red-winged Parrot has an extensive distribution across northern and northeastern Australia, mainly in the arid interior but extending to the coast in much of the Top End. It occupies most kinds of woodlands with a mean annual rainfall of 400–1,000 mm and it tends to become increasingly uncommon towards either end of this range. In the most arid regions it is largely confined to riverine woodlands. Like most desert birds, it is nomadic, especially at the borders of its distribution.

Easily recognised as the only Australian parrot with bright red wing patches, the sexes are similar, although females are much duller than males. Their diet includes insects, nectar, blossoms, berries, nuts and seeds, and the birds sometimes visit croplands to feed on ripening grain. They seldom fly to the ground except when they come to riverbanks and stock dams to drink.

Who are the 'Magnificent' Parrots?

Regent Parrots feed mainly on grass seed but are not averse to lunching in apple orchards.

*T*he Princess Parrot, the Superb Parrot and the Regent Parrot make up the genus *Polytelis*, a name based on an ancient Greek word meaning 'magnificent' or 'superb'. All three of these species are confined to Australia. One of their most obvious external features is their especially long, slender tails. With the central pair of tail feathers being so very much longer than the others, members of this group have a distinctively long, thin shape. Possibly as a strategy to reduce their visibility these three species share the habit of perching lengthwise along their perch. All inhabitants of arid open woodlands, they are essentially seed eaters. Their bills are small and slender and they forage either on the ground or in trees.

Superb Parrots tend to gather in age-segregated flocks.

Age-segregated Flocks

*A*lthough many parrot species travel around in large flocks for part of their day or at a particular season, few live full-time and all year round in flocks. The Superb Parrot is an exception. These strongly gregarious parrots tend to live in year-round flocks that are segregated by age: young in one flock, adults in another. Young Superb Parrots mainly migrate northwards in autumn but most adults do not travel far from their permanent nesting hollows. During the breeding season in spring and early summer, adult females drop out of the flock to lay their eggs and incubate them alone but two or three times a day, the 'husbands' leave the flock to feed their mates.

Termite Incubators

*M*ost Australian parrots nest in tree hollows but three species — the Golden-shouldered Parrot, the Hooded Parrot and the probably extinct Paradise Parrot — nest exclusively in the mounds of termites. Working together in shifts, the pair dig a tunnel about half a metre long into the mound with their strong bills and at the end they excavate a chamber to hold their clutch of 4–6 eggs. This is more work than simply commandeering a hole in a tree but it does have the advantage of exploiting the termite's own 'air-conditioning' skills. The temperature inside a termite's mound is remarkably constant and this means that eggs need less incubation and chicks need less constant brooding.

> **CLEANSING CATERPILLAR**
> In the termite mounds where Golden-shouldered Parrots nest lives a species of tiny moth whose caterpillars eat the chicks' droppings and keep the nest clean.

How do Desert Parrots Deal with Drought?

*T*here are two broad strategies for coping with a desert environment, where resources of all kinds are scarce. One might be summarised as: spread thin, dig in, live long enough to profit from mistakes and make do with less. The lifestyle of Major Mitchell's Cockatoo comes close to this option. The second strategy however, is better suited to Australia's erratic 'boom' and 'bust' cycles of drought and flood. Many birds organise their lives as though in obedience to the following set of commands: when rains do occur, find the spot quickly, get there quickly, breed quickly for as long as the good times last, then scatter. This is a ruthless and demanding lifestyle but it seems to work. Several Australian parrots have evolved as specialists in this respect, most notably the Princess Parrot and the Scarlet-chested Parrot.

Parrots in arid regions, like these Bluebonnets and Mulga Parrots, rely on artificial water sources.

Princess Parrot   40 cm

A vision in multicoloured pastel shades, the Princess Parrot is one of Australia's least known birds.

Often known as Alexandra's Parrot, the Princess Parrot is a scarce nomad of the most arid mulga and spinifex scrubs of the northern deserts. It is one of the most elusive of all Australian birds.

Typically a flock appears in a grove of trees along some dry riverbed, spends several months in the region, raises a brood of young, then vanishes again into the desert. It is seldom reported, and even today, almost nothing is known of its habits and behaviour in the wild. Paradoxically, it does well in captivity if properly cared for and it is popular and well established as an aviary bird.

The delicate pastel hues of the Princess Parrot are unique among parrots. Males have light blue crowns, pink throats and light yellow underparts, with greenish yellow shoulder patches. Females are similar but duller.

MYSTERIOUS ORNAMENT

Adult male Princess Parrots have a curious decoration on each wingtip. Counting from the outermost, the third primary feather — which in this species happens to be the longest wing feather — flares abruptly at its tip to form a small, spoon-shaped elongation. Its purpose is entirely unknown.

An Elusive Parrot

The Princess Parrot feeds mainly on seeds, especially of spinifex, as well as fruits and blossoms. The bird is so rarely reported that its status is very difficult to assess and it may be declining. Occasionally single birds are reported but more often Princess Parrots travel and feed in small flocks of perhaps 10–20 birds. They usually nest in groups and on several occasions five or more nests have been found in a single tree. In keeping with their nomadic lifestyle, they stay in an area only long enough to breed and they usually leave as soon as the young can fly.

The male Superb Parrot's head is boldly marked with yellow.

Superb Parrot   40 cm

The Superb Parrot's distribution once extended into Victoria but since European settlement it has steadily declined, especially in the south and it is now effectively confined to New South Wales. This decline seems to be associated with the destruction of the once widespread forests of River Red Gums upon which the bird relies for nesting.

The adult male is bright green and readily identifiable by its bright yellow face and crown, with a band of scarlet across the upper breast. Females have plain green heads. Their warbling calls have a distinctive husky quality.

Superb Parrots breed in the riverside forests of the Murray, Edwards, Murrumbidgee and Lachlan Rivers in the region approximately bounded by Deniliquin and Cowra. In winter, much of the population disperses northwards to the general vicinity of Coonabarabran in north-central New South Wales.

Bright yellow wings patches identify the male Regent Parrot but females are mainly dull olive.

Regent Parrot   39–41 cm

The Regent Parrot is widespread in southwestern Australia and it also inhabits parts of the southeast, especially mallee country near the Murray River where the boundaries of Victoria, South Australia and New South Wales come together. With the development of agriculture in the west, the populations of the Regent Parrot at first rose in numbers, presumably because stock dams provided a source of water where previously there had been none. In recent decades, however, the increase has been reversed, possibly as additional clearing reduced the supply of suitable nesting sites.

Regent Parrots are unmistakable. Males are mainly rich yellow in plumage with red secondary feathers and large yellow wing patches. Females are similar in pattern but mainly dull olive in colour. Eastern males are usually more richly coloured than western males. Immature males take about 14 months to acquire their adult plumage.

Red-capped Parrot

33–37 cm

At a distance the Red-capped Parrot is easily identified by its distinctive yellow-green rump, a feature especially obvious in flight. Close up, adult males show a unique combination of red crown, yellow-green cheeks, deep blue breast and red undertail coverts. Females and young birds are similar but much duller.

The Red-capped Parrot is confined to the southwestern corner of the Australian continent. Its distribution and its lifestyle are both strongly associated with a single species of eucalypt, the marri, which is also confined to southwestern Australia. Marri seeds are an important food for the Red-capped Parrot, although it also eats other kinds of seeds as well as fruit, nectar, buds and flowers. It can quite often be seen on the ground gathering grass seeds and it sometimes makes a nuisance of itself in orchards. The Red-capped Parrot remains common within its restricted distribution, perhaps partly encouraged by the widespread planting of marri as a suburban shade tree in many cities and towns.

The deep blue breast is this parrot's most distinctive feature but its yellow-green rump is often easier to see.

Special Adaptation

Marri seed pods are shaped like a deep bowl, about 3 cm deep and approximately as broad. The extremely long and pointed upper mandible of the Red-capped Parrot is specially adapted for the extraction of these deeply embedded seeds. Deftly the parrot rotates the fruit in one foot while inserting the tip of its bill into it to nip out the seeds around the edge. This technique improves with practice so that young birds tend to be very much more clumsy than their more experienced elders.

Bluebonnet

28–34 cm

Clad in a basic colour scheme of indigo and pale khaki, no other parrot looks quite like a Bluebonnet. Its plumage differs markedly in detail, however, across the bird's distribution in Australia's southeastern interior. Towards the north of its range in southwestern Queensland the Bluebonnet has clear yellow undertail coverts and dull olive yellow shoulder patches but in the south it has bright red undertail coverts and dull red shoulder patches. Another population is isolated on the Nullarbor Plain; these birds are much smaller and paler with two-tone blue faces, red undertail coverts and red-and-yellow shoulder patches. Whatever the variations, few obvious differences in plumage exist between the sexes or indeed between young birds and adults.

No other Australian parrot shares the Bluebonnet's unique deep blue and dull brown colour scheme.

Habitat and Habits

Bluebonnets are common and widespread in dry open woodlands across much of inland southeastern Australia but they seem to have very specific habitat requirements that are not easy to define because they are often absent from large stretches of country that seem perfectly suitable to any casual observer.

They live in pairs or small parties, seldom forming flocks of any significant size, and they feed on seeds taken mainly on the ground. Here their subdued colouring blends with the background and they are easily overlooked but you usually know when you have entered Bluebonnet country as these birds have a habit of perching conspicuously on fences along the roadside.

FEATHER FEATURES
Bluebonnets have several slight but very unusual plumage features, the functions of which are unknown. For example, their wing feathers are unusually pointed at the tip and those on the crown are unusually long, resulting in a very small but distinct crest which they sometimes raise when agitated.

Red-rumped Parrot   27 cm

Male Red-rumped Parrots are grass-green with a bright red patch on the back.

In Canberra and many other inland towns and cities of the southeast, the Red-rumped Parrot is one of the most familiar urban birds. Small parties or flocks bustle unobtrusively over wasteland, vacant lots, golf courses, the edges of playing fields or the grass verges along roads and railway tracks. Their natural habitat is lightly timbered grasslands, seldom far from water. In more modified grassy habitats, such as on and around the lawns of established garden suburbs, they are seldom seen since they feed almost exclusively on grass seeds, which are rarely allowed to occur due to regular mowing.

GAINING GROUND

The Red-rumped Parrot seems to have increased its range since the turn of the century and is now common in many coastal districts from which it was absent last century. In the vicinity of Sydney, for example, it was unknown before about 1950 but it is now well established in a number of outer western suburbs.

Description and Habits

In flight adult male Red-rumps are unmistakable, with their bright green plumage and small red patch across the lower back but they are more difficult to see while they are foraging. Females have a rather nondescript dull olive colouring and lack obvious markings of any kind. Juvenile birds resemble females.

Red-rumps are sedentary and even winter flocks seldom roam very far from their nesting areas. During the breeding season in spring males often congregate in small flocks while the females are otherwise occupied with incubating eggs or rearing young. Males however do regularly visit their mates to feed them at this time.

Mulga Parrot
28 cm

The Mulga Parrot resembles the Red-rumped Parrot but it usually inhabits drier and harsher country.

As its name suggests, the Mulga Parrot especially favours mulga scrub but it also occurs in all kinds of arid, open woodlands. Like its close relative, the Red-rumped Parrot, it feeds mostly on grass seeds gathered from the ground but while the Red-rumped Parrot appears to have profited from changes since European settlement, Mulga Parrot populations appear to have declined. Although widespread from central New South Wales westwards and all across the southern interior, these parrots are seldom numerous. Little is known of their ecology or the reasons for their increasing scarcity.

Description and Behaviour

In size, shape and general appearance the Mulga Parrot closely resembles the Red-rumped Parrot but the multicoloured male is clad in vivid hues of green, red, blue and yellow. Key identification points to note are the yellow patches on the shoulders and a fleck of red at the back of the head. Females and young birds are drab, although the female often shows a hint of dull orange on her shoulders and nape.

The Mulga Parrot resembles the Red-rumped Parrot in behaviour, too, but it is often even more quiet and unobtrusive. Usually encountered in pairs or family parties, it seldom gathers in large flocks, even in winter. Like so many birds of Australia's arid interior, it is partly nomadic, wandering far in search of food and water during times of drought and nesting whenever local rainfall encourages a crop of grass seeds.

Paradise Parrot   27 cm

This specimen and a few others like it are probably all that remain of the long-lost Paradise Parrot.

If the gorgeous, brightly coloured Paradise Parrot still exists it must be counted among the most elusive of all Australian birds. Nothing at all has been reliably reported about it since the 1920s. At that time a naturalist named C.H. Jerrard observed and photographed Paradise Parrots in the Burnett River district of southern Queensland. In a letter to the prominent ornithologist A. Chisholm in 1936 he recorded the date of 14 November 1927 as his last sighting. Rumours and unsubstantiated reports persist to this day but 1927 still stands as the year of the last confirmed sighting of the mysterious Paradise Parrot.

EXTINCTIONS

If, by some faint chance, the Paradise Parrot still survives, then only two bird species have entirely vanished from the Australian continent since European settlement. These are a couple of emu species that were found isolated on King Island and Kangaroo Island in the late 1700s and they were exterminated almost immediately.

A Speculative Ecology

Although the Paradise Parrot is known to have occurred from central Queensland southwards into northern New South Wales, the full extent of its distribution remains unestablished. Little is known of its life history but it seems to have been very similar to that of the Golden-shouldered Parrot and the Hooded Parrot. Certainly, it shared their dependence on grass seeds and it may well have been the failure of this food supply, brought about by a combination of overgrazing, bush-fires and prolonged drought, that lead to its demise.

Golden-shouldered Parrot   26 cm

Now very rare, the Golden-shouldered Parrot is unusual among Australian parrots in that it nests in termite mounds. Both members of the pair cooperate in drilling a tunnel into the mound, then hollowing out a chamber at the end in which the female lays the 3–6 eggs that form her clutch.

Usually encountered in pairs or small flocks, the Golden-shouldered Parrot has a severely restricted distribution in the interior of Cape York Peninsula, where it favours open savanna woodlands with numerous termite mounds. Its diet consists of grass seeds which it gathers from the ground.

The male is a strikingly beautiful bird, with a rich turquoise head and breast, a black cap, a yellow band across his forehead, a red belly and a big yellow patch on each wing. By

A pair of Golden-shouldered Parrots.

comparison, his mate is nondescript, being mainly light green with a light blue wash on her face and belly and a bronze nape and crown. Immature birds look much like adult females.

Hooded Parrot   26 cm

The Hooded Parrot and the Golden-shouldered Parrot are very closely related and many researchers prefer to regard them as merely forms of a single species. Both birds rely on grass seeds gathered from the ground and live in open savanna woodlands with abundant termite mounds but the Hooded Parrot is confined to the northern part of the Top End, mainly in Arnhem Land.

The colouring of the male Hooded and Golden-shouldered Parrots are similar and at first glance they are hard to tell apart. However, the Hooded Parrot is slightly larger on average and its black cap extends down to its forehead to form a 'hood' of solid colour. Females are also

A male Hooded Parrot.

similar to one another but in the Hooded Parrot the light blue-grey of the face and forehead extends further back onto the crown. Like the Golden-shouldered Parrot, it is elusive and very hard to find.

Extinct or Just Hard to Find?

*H*ow can we be sure that an animal has become extinct? The Night Parrot is a good example of the difficulty inherent in establishing , beyond any doubt that a species is extinct. Its extraordinarily elusive lifestyle and mainly nocturnal habits mean that the bird would be extremely difficult to detect even if it were common. Night Parrots are quite often reported; most sightings are probably valid but they cannot be rigorously checked. One found dead in 1990 by the roadside near Boulia in outback Queensland, apparently killed by a passing vehicle, is the first absolutely irrefutable evidence of its continued existence in more than half a century.

Few scientists have seriously doubted the Night Parrot's continued existence but all attempts to find one alive have failed.

Positive evidence for the existence of the Paradise Parrot has been lacking for nearly as long. Most ornithologists have abandoned hope for the Paradise Parrot but the intensely secretive habits of the Night Parrot make the question of its continued existence very hard to assess. All that can be said is that, so far, all attempts to locate a viable population have failed. If you should be lucky enough to find such a bird, you should contact your State museum or National Parks office.

The Night Parrot's prime habitat consists of spinifex grassland, which covers several million hectares of Australia's arid interior.

ISLAND INVASION

Islands are particularly vulnerable to extinction as any species are unable to escape from introduced pests. On Lord Howe Island, five species of songbirds were lost within a year or two after a ship, the SS *Makambo*, grounded on the island in 1918. Rats on the ship got ashore and soon a plague of them was destroying songbird eggs everywhere on the island.

Maintaining Habitat for the Ground Parrot

*W*hen fire, flood or some similar catastrophe destroys an area of vegetation, the plants subsequently regain lost ground over the following years. A predictable cycle of plant recolonisation occurs: from weeds through to shrubs and finally to forest is one typical pattern. When the original cover is finally restored the resultant vegetation is commonly called climax. Some animals may require climax vegetation for food and shelter while others are dependent on the interim plants of a cycle. The Ground Parrot, for example, needs heathland at that stage of the

The Ground Parrot's status is precarious because of its highly specialised habitat requirements.

succession cycle between three to nine years after a major fire.

Such highly specialised animals often present wildlife managers with a complex problem. It is not enough to merely put aside a section of habitat for the species as this habitat is constantly undergoing change. In order to fully protect the animals, it is necessary to skilfully manipulate the habitat to ensure that at least some parts of it remain suitable. In the case of Ground Parrots, this is done by a carefully orchestrated sequence of controlled burnings, producing a sort of mosaic of heathland in various stages of recovery after fire.

Which Australian Parrot Builds its Own Nest?

*M*ost Australian parrots do not build their own nests. They prefer the prefab homes afforded by old hollow trees. The Ground Parrot is exceptional in

Unusual among Australian parrots, the Ground Parrot builds its own nest, a saucer of grass stalks in dense cover.

this respect. Come spring it scrapes a shallow saucer-shaped depression in the ground and lines it with plant stems and leaves. The nest is always well hidden in dense cover, often tucked up against a grass tussock. The female lays 3–4 round, white eggs and incubates them over a period of about 21 days. During this time the attentive male will ply her with food. The young usually leave the nest a week or so before they fledge at about 30 days.

Swift Parrot

23–26 cm

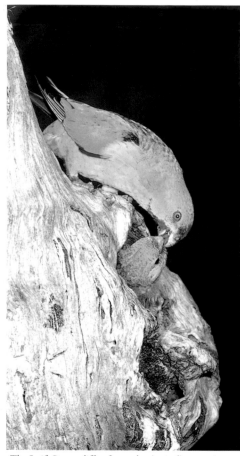

The Swift Parrot is a typical parrot in ancestry but in many ways it more strongly resembles a lorikeet. Like lorikeets — but unlike most parrots — it is noisy and conspicuous when feeding. As its name suggests, it has the swift, rocketing flight so characteristic of lorikeets. It also feeds mainly on nectar and pollen, occasionally supplementing its diet with insects or their larvae. Like the lorikeets, too, it is very much a bird of the treetops, although it often visits the ground to drink.

Even its pointed tail and multicoloured plumage might suggest the features of a lorikeet. The head and body are mostly green but it has red underwings and there are patches of bright red on the forehead, chin and shoulders. The eyes are yellow and the bill is pale grey. The sexes are similar.

The Swift Parrot differs from other 'typical' parrots in relying heavily on a diet of nectar, just like the lorikeets.

Migration and Status

The Swift Parrot is one of the few migratory parrots. It nests only in Tasmania, generally from October to December, and in autumn it migrates across Bass Strait to spend the winter roaming the eucalypt woodlands of southeastern Australia. In its wanderings it sometimes strays as far north as Mackay in Queensland or as far west as Adelaide but the bulk of the wintering population is more or less confined to Victoria.

Its status has been a matter of concern for some years. Populations seem to be declining, perhaps because of reduced supplies of nectar resulting from the clearing and general degradation of southeastern forests. This species now appears on the endangered species list in several States.

Budgerigar
18 cm

*The original wild Budgerigar is mainly green and yellow
(above), with very subtle differences between the sexes (right).*

As a familiar household pet, the Budgerigar
may well be the best-known bird in the world
next to the street pigeon. Many domestic strains are pale blue, yellow or even
white but wild birds are mainly green with a yellow head.

Wild Populations

Although Budgerigars sometimes occur in very large flocks, they are more
usually encountered in groups of perhaps a 100 birds or so. Strongly nomadic,
they travel virtually everywhere across the
continent except for the forested areas of the
east coast, the far north and the southwest.
Lost pets and escaped cage birds are a
frequent sight in eastern towns and cities but
wild Budgerigars do not normally venture
across the Great Dividing Range. There is a
strong seasonal bias in their movements,
which tend southwards in spring and
northwards in autumn.

With their bright green breasts, yellow
heads and closely barred necks, wild
Budgerigars are almost unmistakable. Their
calls include a characteristic warbling twitter,
easily recognised once learned. They feed on
grass seeds gathered from the ground and
nest in hollow trees.

> **BUDGIE HORDES**
>
> It has been said that the
> Budgerigar may be Australia's
> most numerous parrot and some
> accounts speak of 'vast hordes
> darkening the sky'; others tell of
> branches 4 cm in diameter
> breaking under the weight of
> densely packed perching birds.
> There are also accounts of birds
> coming to a waterhole so eager
> to drink that they simply
> splashed down into the water,
> only to be drowned by others
> following in their wake.

Ground Parrot

29–30 cm

The Ground Parrot has unusually precise habitat requirements. Optimum habitat is low, dense heathlands between about three and nine years after a fire. As banksias and other trees gradually recover, the environment becomes unacceptable to Ground Parrots, who then disperse in search of other suitable habitat.

Because of the Ground Parrot's very specific needs, its distribution is patchy across coastal and near-coastal parts of southeastern Australia. In addition to heathlands, it is also abundant on the extensive buttongrass plains of western Tasmania and this indeed remains its stronghold. There is also a population on the coastal heaths of the far southwest of Western Australia but little is known of its status.

True to its name, the Ground Parrot is very difficult to observe because it seldom leaves dense groundcover.

Elusive Ground-dwellers

It is very difficult to actually find Ground Parrots. They seldom perch anywhere but on the ground in dense cover, where they feed on a variety of plant items including buds and seeds. Although extraordinarily secretive and elusive, they are largely active by day, not nocturnal as was once believed. The best way of locating them is to visit a likely stretch of heath on a calm, sunny evening in spring. If the parrots are there, come sundown the males are likely to announce their territorial holdings with a distinctive series of three or four high-pitched, clear and mellow whistles.

The Ground Parrot is almost unique among Australian parrots in that it nests on the ground. It scrapes a shallow saucer-shaped depression in the ground and lines it with plant stems, stalks and leaves. The nest is always well hidden in dense cover, often tucked up against a grass tussock.

> **COUNTING PARROTS**
> One way of finding Ground Parrots is to put your name forward as a volunteer helper for the regular censuses conducted on this parrot by researchers at several of its known localities, such as Barren Grounds National Park in eastern New South Wales.

Night Parrot   23 cm

The Night Parrot is similar to the Ground Parrot but it lacks any trace of red on its forehead.

In many ways the Night Parrot is the yeti of Australian birds. In all the museums of the world there are only 23 known specimens. Despite persistent sight reports and rumours, a specimen taken in 1912 was, until recently, the last concrete, irrefutable evidence of its existence.

In 1990, however, a specimen was found dead by a roadside in outback Queensland and unverified sightings continue to be reported at the rate of several per year. Nevertheless, the question of the Night Parrot's present status remains one of the most tantalizing mysteries among Australian birds.

Piecing Together the Evidence

The Night Parrot is, or was, a small yellowish green bird with intricate yellow, black and dark brown markings. It was once widely distributed across the arid interior of the continent. Knowledge of its biology is fragmentary at best: almost everything that is known was recorded last century by an early naturalist, F W. Andrews. Working in the vicinity of Lake Eyre and the Gawler Ranges for the South Australian Museum during the 1870s, Andrews collected 16 specimens of the parrot. In 1867 one was dispatched to London Zoo but it lived for only a few months.

From this early documentation it appears that the Night Parrot spends all day in the heart of a clump of spinifex, emerging only after dark to visit the nearest waterhole to drink. Early accounts claimed that it bit off spinifex stems to form a tunnel, then pulled them back into place to conceal the entrance. Several calls were described, including a low, two-syllable or prolonged and mournful whistle, and a croaking alarm call. The Night Parrot is known to feed mainly on spinifex seeds but many early records mention its occurrence in samphire flats around salt lakes.

How do Parrots Moult?

A bird's feathers ultimately wear out and must be shed and replaced. This process is known as a moult and in all birds it takes place at least once a year. In parrots, a moult usually occurs just after breeding, although in many species the process is so extended that the last feathers of one moult may be still emerging as the first feathers of the succeeding moult are being shed. A moult is intricate and almost invariant: a parrot's

This moult is heavily influenced by illness. Normally the process shows few external signs of progress.

10 primary feathers, for example, are shed in a constant sequence from the centre of the wing outwards in both directions.

Do Parrots have Enemies?

N ot many compared to numerous other birds. Small parrots, of course, are more vulnerable than larger ones but generally speaking the combination of large size, a formidable bill, a pugnacious disposition and strongly social habits render many parrots relatively immune from all but the largest and most skilful predators. Parrots are also intelligent and long-lived, which gives them a decided advantage in learning to avoid the varied threats of their environment. Peregrine Falcons often take Galahs and the larger owls may be a threat at night but for the most part the larger cockatoos especially have little to fear from anything in the Australian bush.

A Brown Falcon wheels to attack. Falcons are among the few serious predators of Australian parrots.

BABY PARROTS
Nearly naked when they first hatch, baby parrots are sparsely clad in fluffy down. The down of many species is white but in most cockatoos it is yellow, in Galahs it is pink, and in Ground Parrots it is a sooty black.

A Checklist of Australian Parrots

Below is a complete list of all parrot species recorded in Australia and its territories. Because common names often vary, the scientific name is also given to help you find a species in publications using different common names.

FAMILY CACATUIDAE (COCKATOOS)

Palm Cockatoo *Probosciger atterimus*
Red-tailed Black-Cockatoo
    Calyptorhynchus banksii
Glossy Black-Cockatoo *Calyptorhynchus
    lathami*
Yellow-tailed Black-Cockatoo
    Calyptorhynchus funereus
Short-billed Black-Cockatoo
    Calyptorhynchus latirostris
Long-billed Black-Cockatoo
    Calyptorhynchus baudinii
Gang-gang Cockatoo *Callocephalon
    fimbriatum*
Galah *Cacatua roseicapilla*
Long-billed Corella *Cacatua tenuirostris*
Western Corella *Cacatua pastinator*
Little Corella *Cacatua sanguinea*
Major Mitchell's Cockatoo *Cacatua
    leadbeateri*
Sulphur-crested Cockatoo *Cacatua
    galerita*
Cockatiel *Nymphicus hollandicus*

FAMILY PSITTACIDAE (PARROTS)

SUBFAMILY LORIINAE (LORIKEETS)
Rainbow Lorikeet *Trichoglossus
    haematodus*
Scaly-breasted Lorikeet *Trichoglossus
    chlorolepidotus*
Varied Lorikeet *Psitteuteles versicolor*
Musk Lorikeet *Glossopsitta concinna*
Little Lorikeet *Glossopsitta pusilla*
Purple-crowned Lorikeet *Glossopsitta
    porphyrocephala*

SUBFAMILY PSITTACINAE ('TYPICAL' PARROTS)
Eclectus Parrot *Eclectus roratus*
Australian King-Parrot *Alisterus
    scapularis*
Double-eyed Figparrot *Cyclopsitta
    diophthalma*

Red-cheeked Parrot *Geoffroyus geoffroyi*
Red-winged Parrot *Aprosmictus
    erythropterus*
Red-capped Parrot *Purpureicephalus
    spurius*
Bluebonnet *Northiella haematogaster*
Swift Parrot *Lathamus discolor*
Budgerigar *Melopsittacus undulatus*
Ground Parrot *Pezoporus wallicus*
Night Parrot *Pezoporus occidentalis*
Superb Parrot *Polytelis swainsonii*
Regent Parrot *Polytelis anthopeplus*
Princess Parrot *Polytelis alexandrae*
Red-rumped Parrot *Psephotus
    haematonotus*
Mulga Parrot *Psephotus varius*
Golden-shouldered Parrot *Psephotus
    chrysopterygius*
Hooded Parrot *Psephotus dissimilis*
Paradise Parrot (probably extinct)
    Psephotus pulcherrimus
Red-crowned Parrakeet *Cyanoramphus
    novaezelandiae*
Norfolk Island Kaka (extinct) *Nestor
    productus*
Green Rosella *Platycercus caledonicus*
Crimson Rosella *Platycercus elegans*
Eastern Rosella *Platycercus eximius*
Pale-headed Rosella *Platycercus adscitus*
Northern Rosella *Platycercus venustus*
Western Rosella *Platycercus icterotis*
Australian Ringneck *Barnardius zonarius*
Bourke's Parrot *Neopsephotus bourkii*
Blue-winged Parrot *Neophema
    chrysostoma*
Elegant Parrot *Neophema elegans*
Rock Parrot *Neophema petrophila*
Orange-bellied Parrot *Neophema
    chrysogaster*
Turquoise Parrot *Neophema pulchella*
Scarlet-chested Parrot *Neophema
    splendida*

INDEX